# With you Always

Daily Meditations on the Gospels

# With you Always

Francis X. Gaeta

**ave maria press**   Notre Dame, Indiana

All royalties from this book are dedicated to the ministry of St. Brigid's Parish Outreach, Westbury, New York.

International Standard Book Number: 0-87793-946-2

Cover and text design by Katherine Robinson Coleman

Printed and bound in the United States of America.

*Library of Congress Cataloging-in-Publication Data*
Gaeta, Francis X.
With you always : daily meditations on the Gospels / Francis X. Gaeta.
        p. cm.
    Includes bibliographical references.
    ISBN 0-87793-946-2 (pbk.)
      1. Church year meditations. 2. Bible. N.T. Gospels--Meditations. 3.
Catholic Church--Prayer-books and devotions--English. I. Title.
BX2170.C55G34 2000
242'.3--dc21
                                    00-008886
                                         CIP

*I lovingly dedicate this book*

*to the memory*

*of*

*my dear parents*

*Pasquale (Pat) Gaeta and Agnes Miller*

*who taught me everything I know*

*and who made sure that each day*

*at 188 Skillman St., 316 Willoughby Ave.,*

*and 90 Lake Shore Dr.*

*was never ordinary*

*but always*

*extraordinary.*

# Contents

# *Preface*

My dear friends,

This book really began in 1966 when as a young priest I met one of the greatest people in my life, Sr. Thelma Hall, r.c. Thelma guided me at the Ronkonkoma Cenacle in my first directed retreat. I have never recovered!

She led me to the word of God and helped me to pray with the scriptures for the first time. She introduced me to *lectio divina*, the prayerful meditative reading and praying of the scriptures.

This book is the natural evolution of what began way back when! It is my reaction to, praying of, and response to the daily bread of the gospels of ordinary time. The gospels of Advent, Christmas, Lent, and Easter—which include the birth narratives and Jesus' passion—are not treated here; rather, this book focuses on Jesus in his public ministry.

This book is intended for those interested in praying daily on the gospels. It is organized according to the daily readings of the lectionary. It is meant to be a springboard for personal prayer. It should prove helpful for those who preach on the lectionary each day, as well as for those looking for "daily bread" for their personal prayer.

I pray with you that the Lord will lead us to the mystery of his love which is, as Sr. Thelma Hall's book tells us, *Too Deep for Words*.

In Christ's love,

Frank Gaeta

*The*
*Gospel*
*According*
*to*
*Mark*

# Jesus Calls the First Disciples

## MARK 1:14-20

*Monday of the First Week of the Year*

We begin this first week with Jesus calling Peter, Andrew, James, and John. "Come after me; I will make you fishers of men." The command of Jesus has such excitement and youthful enthusiasm about it. It seems to be fun to leave boat and nets and even family behind to follow Jesus and to be counted as one of his disciples.

We are always so encouraged when we meet a minister who has that youthful enthusiasm for the Lord's work, especially an older person in whom the fire has never given out. What a blessing it is for the church to have ministers who still get a kick out of ministry and being with people.

The call of Jesus is not just the lot of the young. We are all constantly being called. We are being invited to say our own "yes" to the Lord in new and constantly changing ways. Marriage, priesthood, single life, religious life, and deaconate are the usual ways in which we understand call or vocation. In reality, the events of our lives are the ongoing revelation of the call and will of God for us. There is nothing tidy or static about vocation.

The call to marriage becomes quite different when children come along and new parents are beckoned to a deeper generosity than they have ever known. Children grow and parents deal with their growth. Sickness, teenage years, and religious and psychological development present parents with new and undreamed of occasions to say "yes" to what becomes many new calls with the passing of time.

How difficult it is to continue to say the "yes" in a strained or problem marriage. How hard couples have to work when the glow of romantic love ebbs and life becomes hard and joyless work. How hard that "yes" becomes when a couple, after long and deep soul-searching, realizes that the new vocation they must embrace is divorce.

So many events will be the opportunity to respond to the call of Jesus. Are we always going to be able to make the right decision? The right decision is embracing what we in our hearts truly believe to be the Lord's will. Through prayer, reflection, and direction we choose "our" best. When we do so, it will always be the "right" decision.

Christian decision-making isn't just a response to a crisis. Christian decision-making is the day-in and day-out walking with the Lord, and holding up our own life and decisions to him each day. We really cannot make the "major" decisions of life as disciples unless we have been making the nitty-gritty ones each and every day with him. Our decisions flow from our intimate and constant relationships with Jesus. We believe him when he tells us that without him we can do nothing.

## Jesus Drives Out an Unclean Spirit

MARK 1:21-28

*Tuesday of the First Week of the Year*

As the people listen to Jesus, they comment that he teaches with authority. So much of the ministry of Jesus centered around teaching. He moved from place to place. His pulpit was any place he could gather a few people together. Whether in a boat on the Sea of Galilee or on the slope of the Mount of the Beatitudes, Jesus was at his best when he could gather around him people who were looking for something to put their faith in. Jesus was a rabbi. He taught by word, but most of all, he taught by example.

Jesus preaches in a new and revolutionary way. He preaches with authority. Authority is not power. Power flows from things outside ourselves such as money, weapons, armies, and titles. Authority flows from what is within us—love, integrity, and truth. The words of Jesus touch and transform hearts because his words are an extension of all he is and all he possesses. Jesus has no need of any external forces to touch people. He doesn't force or coerce anyone to do anything.

The love that flows from him is the soul of his authority. His words become irresistible because he himself is the word of love that his hearers experience. Jesus is in constant union with his Father. The word he speaks is the Holy Spirit, the love of the Father and the Son. This word is life, holiness, and love. It is the word of authority.

People like Dorothy Day, Cardinal Bernardin, Pope John XXIII, Pope John Paul II, and Mother Teresa speak with authority. The inner core of truth and beauty shines forth in their lives and in their words. They are the sermon that is being preached! They have allowed the Holy Spirit to fill them so that they have become the vessels of God's love and God's authority.

There are so many beautiful and loving people in the world who speak with great authority because they are the vessels of God's love. They shine in the beauty of God's truth and in all that they are. They are the living word of Jesus' life and love.

Let us speak, preach, teach, and live with the authority of Jesus—the authority of love, integrity, and truth. Let us never underestimate the power of our testimony. The day-in and day-out fidelity that children experience in their parents literally molds, directs, and creates their hearts and consciences. The faithful witness and care of a teacher, priest, or sister deeply influences the life and heart of so many youth.

The world yearns for real role models, people who have tremendous authority because they are there for what they can give, not for what they can get.

## Healing at Peter's Home

MARK 1:29-39

*Wednesday of the First Week of the Year*

The story of the curing of Peter's mother-in-law is always good for a chuckle when a preacher assures his congregation that Peter didn't speak to Jesus for a week because he cured the good lady! All kidding aside, in its own way this gospel passage speaks volumes about the man Peter.

We can only speculate about the details, but it seems pretty certain to me that if Peter lived with his mother-in-law, there must have been a Mrs. Pope and, if you will, lots of little Popes running around. Peter for me becomes so much more believable when I think of him as a family man with a wife and children and mother-in-law he loved deeply.

Peter welcomes Jesus into his home. This home, like all homes, hopefully is not just a house, a place in which to live—but a home, a place to be nurtured, loved, and refreshed. Peter welcomes Jesus into a community of love, his family. In that context, just like in the home of Lazarus, Jesus is allowed to be himself. He is allowed to be human. He is allowed to relate to a family not as the rabbi but as a dear friend. There is no need of religion talk or temple politics talk, just human conversation. This family setting will do much more for Jesus than Jesus will be able to do for them. The Son of Man needs these people more than they need him. He needs to be comforted, encouraged, and loved for who he is and not for what he can do for them. The healer needs to be healed. It is a loving family that has the power to do that.

That's what family does for everyone. To be a part of a family, even for the Son of God, is to be made vulnerable and to experience the most deeply religious experience in life—the love of family. That experience for Jesus and for everyone makes us human, real and in touch with the yearnings of everyone's heart—the need to love and be loved.

After sharing the eucharist of the family meal prepared by mom in the home of Mr. and Mrs. Pope and company, Jesus is ready to embrace the sick, the afflicted, and the possessed. All in need of love come to Jesus and he is able to love them because he has first experienced love, his Father's love and his friend Peter's family's love. That's what family does to us.

## The Cleansing of a Leper

MARK 1:40-45

*Thursday of the First Week of the Year*

The leper approaches Jesus with a plea to be made whole, to be cured. What a wonderful moment of grace it was for this poor person. He disregarded all the taboos and prejudices of his society against him. He would not cry out, "Unclean, unclean!" He would not ring the warning bell hanging around his neck. He ignored the orders of all the "clean" ones around him and would not be silent. He knelt down before Jesus, taking the biggest chance of his life, and simply said: "If you will to do so, you can cure me."

Is not that simple, humble, and sincere prayer a model of what our prayer and everyone's prayer should be like? It is the prayer of the leper. There are so many lepers in the church today, those made so by their own self-hatred and those made to feel like lepers by the church and society.

So many feel like lepers because of guilt they carry about. So many feel they are unworthy of the forgiveness and mercy of Jesus because of their past and thus struggle in the present. Some who bear the pain of an abortion feel they can never really be forgiven and be a part of the church's life. They feel their sin is unforgivable. People whose marriages have failed sometimes feel that they are condemned to be second-class citizens in a church where only the "perfect" really belong. Persons dealing with addictions of all kinds often feel unwelcome and believe that they can only be part of the team when they clean up their act. They often feel that they don't belong because they're not "all together."

The church of sinners comes across as the judgmental church of the elite. There are so many who feel left out and unwelcome at the table. The poor, the crippled, the blind, the lepers, and the prostitutes are the most important members of the church. They are the ones for whom Jesus has come. They are the ones for whom the church exists, not to condemn, point fingers, or judge, but to embrace lovingly.

We have all felt at one time or another like that leper in the gospel. Let us help and encourage one another to kneel in faith and love before Jesus and pray, "If you will to do so, you can cure me." As we say our prayer, let's look around the table and realize that everyone is in the same boat we're in. Everyone is a sinner, doesn't belong, and is afraid that the group will find out about them and throw them out! Don't be afraid. As we gather at the table, we'll all say the words together: "Lord, I am not worthy . . . only say the word and I shall be healed. Amen!"

# The Healing of a Paralytic

*Friday of the First Week of the Year*

This gospel is a classic! They just will not leave Jesus alone—lowering the paralytic through the roof so that Jesus will heal him! It's Jesus' own fault. That's what he gets for loving people and showing them the power of that love. The dilemma of Jesus is the dilemma of any of his true disciples. Tremendous, and sometimes unreasonable, demands are made upon us. The meaning of our lives is ministering to others.

The life of a parent, spouse, priest, and friend must always be defined in the loving and generous gift of our talents and time to others. It is true that we must care for ourselves, but the meaning and the joy of our lives will come from the gift of ourselves to others. We are called like Jesus *to* serve, not to *be* served. Once we start, there is no stopping.

Notice what the Lord says to the paralytic in the gospel. After he heals him he gives him a job—pick up your mat, go home; get on with your life; start healing others. That's how it is with us. He heals us, he loves us, and then he gives us a job—to do the same for others, to give the gifts away. The next time someone removes the tiles from your roof to place someone at your feet for healing, just remember how they did it to Jesus and chuckle as you remember that you're only getting what you asked for!

At the heart of every Christian vocation there must be passion for service and love of people. The real parent, the real priest, the real friend lives a life of interruptions, inconvenience, hard work, and total giving for others. It is a real sign of death and sickness of the spirit when our main concern becomes our own convenience rather than the pain and need of others.

19

Nothing draws people to Jesus more than the open and loving arms of his ministers welcoming and calling others. How blessed the church is whenever ministers will cheerfully "do windows"!

When we get discouraged we think of the moving scene of Jesus washing the feet of the apostles at the Last Supper, and we remind ourselves that that is the meaning of our call—to wash the feet of one another in Jesus' name.

## Jesus Calls Levi

MARK 2:13-17

*Saturday of the First Week of the Year*

Levi drops his cash box and follows Jesus. He will never be the same again. He heard the call and he had no choice but to respond.

Levi reminds us that Jesus has entered into all of our lives, and he has said those words that change everything: "Come, follow me." Levi was the most unlikely person to be called by Jesus. He was a "sinner." He did one of those jobs that placed him on the outs with the religious folk.

We sometimes feel that we're on the outs. We're not good enough or holy enough to be called by Jesus. Our life is not important or significant enough. When we begin to see our importance as Jesus does, we then begin to hear the call. That call is always there, but we drown it out with our frenetic activity and feelings of unworthiness. When we believe we are loved, we begin to hear this call.

Jesus is calling each of us—just like Levi. He calls us by name. He invites us to leave behind and drop what is not of his Kingdom. He invites us to discover and embrace his presence and his call in all the events and circumstances of our lives. He invites us to embrace him in all our responsibilities, struggles, joys, happiness, and challenges. Jesus' mark is on everything in our lives if we can take the time to really look and find him.

What a great party follows Levi's call! Jesus is there doing what he seems to do best. He eats and drinks, talks, jokes with and probably sings with tax collectors, sinners, soldiers, and prostitutes. What upsets the scribes is what his eating with someone means. For the Jewish people of that time, eating with someone was an act of intimacy. You eat only with those you deeply respect and love.

That's what Jesus' eating with the sinners meant. Jesus was saying with this sign that he loved and embraced and wanted to belong to them. No one was excluded by Jesus. Everyone had a place. Everyone was loved. Everyone belonged.

Jesus continues to invite the sinners, you and me, to his dinner party. We call it the eucharist. It's the one place where everyone belongs and no one can be excluded. Look around. There we all are—the tax collectors, the prostitutes, the blind, the lepers, the crippled, the beggars. We all sit down to eat with the Lord. We are in very good company.

The eucharist, just like the dinner party at Levi's, is not a reward for those who are perfect. It is rather the encouragement and the loving embrace of those who are struggling and trying so hard to follow Jesus. We all fall and fail. Jesus, our loving physician, is there to pick us up and sit us down with him at his table so that we might eat and drink with him once again. That's what really is happening at Mass on Sunday. *Bon Appetit!*

# The Question About Fasting

MARK 2:18-22

*Monday of the Second Week of the Year*

People were questioning Jesus and his disciples about why they did not fast like the disciples of John and the Pharisees. But what they were actually asking was simply this: "Why are you not religious?" "Why have you not adopted a penitential and prayerful lifestyle like the others who always look and act religious?" "Why are you just like us laymen and not set apart like the others?"

These are all very telling questions and they are still difficult for us to answer. For Jesus, faith and love did not consist of externals. It was the heart that really counted. Jesus did not wear a Roman collar or religious habit. He did not live a monastic life. He was simple in lifestyle but certainly not destitute. Jesus was very much bourgeois like us.

Jesus' main mode of ministry was table fellowship. He went anywhere he was invited. He dined with anyone and he ate whatever was put before him. There was no ceremony with him, except the basic courtesy and respect that every human being demands and deserves. Jesus' manner was very ordinary. There was no pretension. There was no seeking after comfort or privilege. Externally Jesus looked and acted like any decent and good man.

It is from this humble vessel that the richness of the Father's love is poured out. The heart of Jesus is his love of the Father and humanity. Nothing gets in the way of truth. To listen to Jesus is to hear the simple and straightforward message of love and change of heart.

The disciple of Jesus quickly learns that holiness comes not from what one does or does not eat, not from what one does or does not wear, and not from how long or in what position one prays. Holiness comes only from loving God and our neighbor as Jesus loved them and as he taught us to love.

As we look into our own hearts, it becomes disturbing how much true holiness we discard because we are clutching to external forms. We and our church are always being challenged to cast aside what is not of God and to grasp what is truly of God—love, truth, justice, and mercy.

We all face the temptation of fasting from food and drink while ignoring the areas of our hearts that yearn for the healing touch of Jesus. Sometimes religion becomes the greatest enemy of faith and love. Let it not be true for us.

The doing of the "things" can distract us from looking at God and at ourselves and asking the real questions about life, love, and salvation. The busyness of religion can make so much noise that we can't hear the gentle voice calling us.

## The Sabbath

MARK 2:23-28

*Tuesday of the Second Week of the Year*

"The sabbath was made for man, not man for the sabbath." Jesus continues what we saw in yesterday's gospel. He continues to teach about the new wine and the need for new wineskins. He teaches a new and radical religion—a religion of the heart that supersedes the religion of tradition.

In so many instances good and faithful Christians form their consciences after careful and sincere reflection and prayer. Their consciences sometimes do not jive with church practice and teaching. Jesus seems to leave room for such things when he pulls the rug out from under some very sacred practices of the Jewish faith. He places a lot of importance on individual experience, circumstances, and decisions, and most of all prayerful discernment.

The religion of Jesus will not be neat and tidy. He seems to have ruled out that kind of thing as we read in yesterday's and today's gospel. Jesus didn't just exempt himself from personal observance, but rather he seemed to be giving new principles of interpretation to his disciples and followers.

In the faithful following of Jesus, much more depends upon the truthful, honest, and loving adaptations of the principles than upon slavish obedience to law. To be faithful, one must always be in the process of personal growth and prayerful discernment of one's personal life and the will of God.

These days remind us of how much we need the help and guidance of the Holy Spirit, and of how Jesus has promised us his Spirit so that we have help in forming our consciences and walking with him in truth and honesty.

We struggle and at times agonize over the question: "What would Jesus do?" To answer that question and to be faithful to the answer is what discipleship is all about. Sometimes our response is not what the law says, yet we must have the integrity always to respect the law and its place. But we must ultimately be faithful to our conscience.

It's not always easy to be faithful. It is not always easy to follow one's conscience. That is why we must be a church on our knees in constant supplication for the grace of the Holy Spirit so that in all things we can say to Jesus in the power of that Spirit: "Jesus, this is my best."

The church must be the community in which we encourage one another to be the best we are capable of becoming, and it must also be the place where the good faith life decisions of sisters and brothers are respected, even when they differ from ours.

# Healing on the Sabbath

### MARK 3:1-6

*Wednesday of the Second Week of the Year*

"Is it permitted to do a good deed on the sabbath—or an evil one? To preserve life—or to destroy it?" For a third day we are faced with the "religion versus holiness" struggle that Jesus—and you and I—have to face.

This confrontation of the religion of heart and the formal exterior observance devoid of interior redemption was made so clear to me as I finished reading Frank McCourt's *Angela's Ashes.*

With the exception of two kind confessors, every religious figure in the memoir was externally perfect in observing religious formality, but internally devoid of the very essentials of the gospel—mercy, compassion, tenderness, forgiveness, and understanding.

Religion for the young boy growing up presented a God of wrath, punishment, severity, and hatred. The religion of Jesus and the God of Jesus was rarely present in the religious experience of this young boy and so many others.

That lack of spirit and heart can also be present in *our* lives when we hide behind legalism and rules to excuse ourselves of what we know Jesus expects of us. The slavish obedience to rules and regulations in seminary and novitiate formation often became the reason for abdicating responsibility and maturity. There was really little difference in intellectual formation and conviction of the "good" seminarian or novice than in the adherents of the doctrine of the Third Reich where the greatest virtue (as sometimes in the church) was obedience and conformity.

The religion of Jesus is a call to personal responsibility, personal growth, and a world-view based on his teaching. It is marked by compassion, mercy, forgiveness, tenderness, and understanding. The new religion of Jesus—freedom and joyful choice of the gospel—places the person and his or her rights above the institution, truth above safety and protecting the institution, and common sense inspired by the Holy Spirit above slavish obedience. Jesus calls us to a new life and we need the new wineskins to contain this new wine.

This spirit of open welcome to all does not mean that we deny our moral teaching. It does mean that *everyone* is welcome whether they keep the rules or not, and that we make God the judge, not ourselves. The church of Jesus is that wonderful and crazy place where everyone sits down together and where everyone belongs. We know that it is not a question of worthiness. That is why saint and sinner celebrate together the wonder and the mystery of being called and loved by the God of mercy.

## The Crowds Follow Jesus

MARK 3:7-12

*Thursday of the Second Week of the Year*

The crowds come to Jesus. They come from all over and they come in great numbers. Why? Because in Jesus Christ, the people sense the presence of God's love among them.

Jesus draws the people to himself—all kinds of people—but most of all the poor, the sinners, the prostitutes, the misfits, the blind, the beggars, and the lepers. In Jesus they have found someone who loves them and accepts them for who they are and does not condemn them.

Jesus is the presence among people of the shalom of God. He is God stretching out his arms to embrace and hold the people he loves so much. He is the gentle suffering servant of Isaiah. He is the one who comes to give the ultimate gift of his own life for the little flock he loves so much.

Jesus is the Good Shepherd seeking out the lost and the lame and the forgotten. He rejoices and calls for a celebration when the stray is found and comes home to take a place at table. He is the Hound of Heaven who never gives up on us but seeks us constantly and without ceasing and is never content until we are in his arms at rest and at peace.

Jesus is the king who chooses to be the servant, the Lord who kneels down to wash and dry our feet. He is the humble servant who tells us that his church is the servant church and that we are called to be servant lovers as he is.

In the transformation of our hearts we become aware that we are called to minister in our home, our church, and our place of work as Jesus did—drawing all people to himself because they see in him God's love in flesh and blood.

Jesus will draw all people to himself when he freely opens his arms on the cross and gives his life for us. When we lay down our life in love for one another then, like Jesus, we will draw all people to ourselves. The reason is simple: love is irresistible.

What a crazy dining room the church is! What a wild and happy meal we celebrate! How could we do otherwise? Everybody is there! Look at us—the saints and sinners; the young and old; married and single; celibate priests and religious; straights and gays; widowed and divorced; single parents; teenagers and middle-aged; the elderly; babies in arms; the mentally and physically challenged; the weeping and laughing. They are all there. They're all us. We're home!

# The Appointing of the Twelve Apostles

MARK 3:13-19

*Friday of the Second Week of the Year*

De gustibus! There's no accounting for taste! Why did he choose these twelve? Here's a better question: Why did he choose us? We don't know, except that he did and that his call is a special facet of his love meant especially and personally for us.

We know that the call has nothing to do with our own personal holiness or worthiness. The call is a gift. The Lord's love is a gift. The fact that he loves us and he calls us does not make us better than anyone else or holier than anyone else. It simply means that he *has* called us. He *does* love us, and he expects us to respond to his call. That call began at baptism and is lived out in so many different ways. It might be marriage, parenthood, divorce, single parenthood, a struggling and painful marriage, single life, the diaconate, being straight or gay. In all these possibilities God is powerfully present and inviting us to find and love him as we love and serve others in our life.

The Lord never withdraws his call or his love. Even when we do not accept it with full and loving hearts, even when we deny and obscure it, he never takes back his love. He never denies the covenant of his love. That covenant was sealed with his blood at the cross. So much of our spiritual life is spent in returning to the covenant over and over again and saying our "yes."

In saying our "yes" we renew our baptism; we renew the life commitment to which God has called us. No matter what the expression of the call becomes as the years pass, the heart of it is always the same: to love God with all our heart, soul, mind, and strength and to love our neighbor as ourselves. The call will always be lived out in healthy, life-giving relationships of love and fidelity.

Right now Jesus calls us: "Come, follow me." Will we have the courage to say "Yes, here I am Lord"? Don't be afraid. He calls because he loves us, and he promises us that he will never abandon us. He will always be there for us.

I read a spoof recently on Jesus' managerial style in choosing the apostles. The Jordan Consulting Firm informed Jesus, in hilarious manner, that all the apostles were first class losers, especially Peter. The only one with any talent, promise, or future in the organization was Judas!

Just remember . . . Jesus called you, and he really does know what he is doing.

## "He Is Out of His Mind"

MARK 3:20-21

*Saturday of the Second Week of the Year*

"He is out of his mind." What a terrible thing for Jesus to hear from his own family and close friends. They don't understand what he is about. They don't know what he is doing. All of a sudden Jesus becomes very much alone, isolated, misunderstood, and afraid. It is one thing when strangers do not understand us, but when our own flesh and blood think we are crazy that's very hard to bear.

When we look closely at the lives of some of our greatest heroes, role models, and saints, we find that most of them had to face a time when they stood all alone and people considered them crazy.

Look at the life of St. Francis when he left his family to marry Lady Poverty. Mother Teresa had to leave the family of the Sisters of Loretto to follow her second call to care for the poorest of the poor. Archbishop Romero never enjoyed the full support of his brother bishops or Rome itself, as he spoke out for the rights of the poor. Pope John XXIII was looked upon as a crazy old man as he announced Vatican II. Dorothy Day was considered unbalanced as she worked for total pacifism and the rights of the poor all through her life.

Almost all of these prophets had to live through the aloneness of being considered out of their minds, just as Jesus was by his family. It seems to go with the territory of being the open vessel waiting to be filled with the spirit of God's love.

If we walk with the Lord, if we live lives of truth, integrity, and justice we can expect that there will be times when even our family of flesh and of the spirit will speak of us as "out of our minds." We can expect no less than what our Jesus received.

As beautiful as discipleship is, it has its price. Dietrich Bonhoeffer wrote *The Cost of Discipleship* in a Nazi prison cell. It cost him his life to be faithful to Jesus, and it will cost each of us to be faithful. Grace is never cheap; sometimes it must be purchased at a great price. It is always worth the price. Always be faithful.

As disciples of Jesus we always have to remember that nothing in this world equals the peace of a good conscience. When we walk in truth and integrity, even when it is painful, we possess a gift that all the money in the world cannot buy—a clear conscience. No one can take that away from us.

## Jesus and Beelzebub

MARK 3:22-30

*Monday of the Third Week of the Year*

We do not know exactly what the sin against the Holy Spirit is. We know that it is a frightening prospect to hear from the lips of Jesus that it is the only unforgivable sin. Can it be that he who comes in flesh and blood to proclaim God's liberality to all of us sets limits to God's mercy and forgiveness?

Perhaps a way to understanding the enormity of the sin against the Holy Spirit is to see it in terms of someone not just making choices against Jesus and his values, but rather deliberately hardening one's heart against Jesus. It appears that was what Jesus experienced in the reaction of the scribes to his ministry when they called him possessed by Beelzebub. They called love "hate" and goodness "evil." They rejected the call and possibility of a new life by embracing death over life.

It seems to imply that the hearers actually had a sense of Jesus' goodness, but to accept it and follow it would mean a total change of heart and life. To preserve what they have, their position and security, they choose to enter the realm of the lie and dwell there.

While we will probably never commit this dreadful sin of totally denying Christ for personal gain, we do fight daily to live in the realm of the truth. We have seen so many of our heroes in government, sports, business, and even the church seem to move from the realm of Truth to the way of the lie. There seems to come over them a transformation in which all reality is jaded and re-created for their own comfort and convenience.

This frightening gospel is a stark reminder to all of us to be people of Truth, which is to say that all of our life and all that we do can be held up to the bright light of Christ's presence. We never hide in the shadows or in the dark because Jesus lights our way and all that we do.

When the Paschal candle is carried into the darkened church on Holy Saturday evening, it is a powerful reminder that Christ's light and love dispels the darkness and that if we live in the light we will never have anything to fear for the Truth does indeed set us free.

# The Family of Jesus

*Tuesday of the Third Week of the Year*

Those of us who love Mary so much find this gospel very harsh: "Who is my mother?" Don't you know, Jesus? Don't you know the one who said "yes" to the angel at the annunciation? Don't you know the one who carried you, gave birth to you, nursed you, and brought you into Egypt? Don't you know the one who cared for your every need and would have been willing to give her life for you at any moment? Don't you know the one who taught you your prayers, your faith, your sensitivity, and your manners? Don't you know the one who taught you how to be human?

Of course you do. It is your mother, Mary.

But now, there is a new order. The least in the Kingdom is more important than even those who are our own flesh and blood. The new life of grace unites us to a new family of love and unity with our God.

The poorest of the poor are now seated at table with you. We are mother and father, sister and brother, parent and child to one another. There is a new family not forged by generations but by the love of God and the blood of the Lamb upon the cross. This new family washes away all the old titles, distinction, and the pecking order of wealth, color, religion, beauty, or giftedness. In this new creation in Christ we are all beautiful in the eyes of our God.

This gospel is not a "put down" of Mary. It is a declaration of our dignity, beauty and worth in the eyes of God. It is a reminder of how we must reverence and cherish ourselves and that we must respond to the miracle of our identity as children of God, God's beloved.

We are also reminded that as we claim our beauty and dignity in God's eyes, we must treat everyone with the same loving respect that we deserve. Our dear sisters and brothers are one with us as Jesus tells us that those who hear the word of God and keep it are mother and family to him.

## The Parable of the Sower

MARK 4:1-20

*Wednesday of the Third Week of the Year*

The Gospel of the Sower is one we've heard so often that it sometimes just doesn't impress us anymore. We've all heard the sermons, and we all know different kinds of soil will predict how well the seed will be able to take root and grow. We have all tried to improve the soil of our hearts so that the pressed down soil of the footpath might become soft, the stones might be removed from the rocky soil, and the thorn bushes might be cut away so that the seed might come to life. We all recognize the challenge that is with us every day until we die: our hearts must be disposed if we are to accept the word of God. Nothing can happen unless we allow it to. The Lord cannot force himself on anyone. We have to want the Lord.

It can become very discouraging to think how little progress we might have made and how far we have to go. It would indeed depress us and discourage us but for one thing: the sower doesn't go out to sow just once. The Lord is constantly sowing the seed of his love. He doesn't come by just once and give up on us because we are not able to absorb his grace and love. The Lord is continuously sowing, calling, coaxing, inviting, and nudging us closer and closer to him.

The embarrassment of this sower is his unfailing and unending love for us. He loves us passionately and without condition. He doesn't love us only when the soil is right. He loves us when we're hard, lifeless, loveless, thorny, and totally self-centered.

The Hound of Heaven pursues us unrelentingly and never gives up until we open our hearts and our arms to his loving embrace. We don't get just one chance with the Lord. Each time he comes by we're just a little bit more able and ready to embrace him and accept him.

How patient he is! How much he loves us! He just never gives up. He keeps coming by; he keeps calling and inviting. He keeps waiting for the day we say to him: "Here I am, Lord."

## A Lamp on a Stand

MARK 4:21-25

*Thursday of the Third Week of the Year*

"In the measure you give you shall receive, and more besides." How much Jesus knows of human nature and life! We can only receive what we give. We can only receive back what we have first given away, and more besides.

Parish life is filled with many touching and beautiful moments. I don't think any touch me as much as when one of the saints of the parish is ill, in trouble, carrying a particularly heavy cross, or even dies. When one of the real disciples of Jesus, whose life has been a celebration of giving everything to others, is in trouble, the outpouring of love toward that person is overwhelming.

The measure they have used to give to others is used for them, and then some! There is no holding back the generosity and love of God's people when they have the opportunity to say "thank you" to the people they know are truly like Christ to others. I suppose you could say that you only get back what you have first given away to others.

How beautiful it is to see the community's response to a young parent's or child's illness. People come out of the woodwork to tell them how much they mean to them and how grateful they are to them.

Standing near the casket with the family of the deceased saint is an incredible privilege as the mourners pass by to pay their respects and speak and console the family. I know I am present at a canonization. Strangers to the family will tell them how their deceased parent or spouse helped them. Families become overwhelmed when they hear the extent of the holiness, love, and generosity of their beloved. It is a very holy moment!

What would I like people to say about me? What would you like to hear? I don't think you and I will care at all about hearing about our accomplishments or our successes. How insignificant it will be to hear about our possessions, wealth, achievements, or honors. All that we will want to hear is people talking about how loving, kind, and generous we were. We will want to hear about what a good person we were, what a good friend, parent, and neighbor we were. We will want to hear someone saying what a difference for good we made in their life.

If we want to be that measure of generosity and love, then we must use that same measure in our dealings with people and in our service to the body of Christ.

## The Growing Seed

MARK 4:26-34

*Friday of the Third Week of the Year*

A man scatters seed on the earth and then goes to bed and gets up day after day and miracles happen! The seed takes root and new life begins, even though he has no idea what is going on or the effect of his action of sowing the seed.

This is the story of countless holy people who are doing an incredible work in proclaiming the word of God in their humble and simple lives and have no appreciation of the power of what they are doing.

This is the story of the parent, priest, CCD teacher, school teacher, parish minister, and countless others who are preaching by the power of their example. Let's think about our CCD teachers and teachers in our Catholic and public schools. So often CCD teachers will pull their hair out in despair or from feelings of failure. So often they will say that they're not accomplishing anything. But they are!

We often never know the good we do in this life. But if we teach our kids and love them and give them the best we have, we are giving them things that we never dreamt of. As poor servants our job is not to be successful (whatever that means) but to be faithful. When we are, the seeds we plant do take root. Sometimes it takes years for them to grow into plants and trees, but grow they will!

Parents teach so much by being faithful and loving to their children. The seeds that are planted *will* come to life. So many hearts of parents are broken when their children drop out of the faith for a while or seem to forget their values. In God's wonderful time, the seeds come to life and bloom into beautiful life-giving trees.

Let us pray not for success but for fidelity. Let us pray that we might love our children even more and never stop giving them our best each and every day. When we do that then we can go to our rest with great confidence, knowing that the seeds we planted will indeed take life and grow into something beautiful for God.

# Jesus Calms the Storm

## MARK 4:35-41

*Saturday of the Third Week of the Year*

It's a bad squall on the Sea of Galilee, the disciples are scared stiff, and Jesus is fast asleep on a cushion no less! What a sight this has to be! The Son of God getting his beauty rest! I wonder if he snored. I'm sure he did. I wonder if he dreamt. You bet he did. About what? All the things you and I dream about, and then some. Jesus is so human. He's so much like us. He *is* one of us. Do you think he was pleasant or a grump when they woke him up? Was he hard to rouse? Definitely, if he slept through a storm!

His lesson of the day was not in calming the storm but in his question addressed to the disciples and to us: "Why are you so afraid? Why is your faith so weak?" Fear flows from a lack of trust and faith in the Lord. As our faith grows, fear should lessen until we reach that point of peace St. John speaks of when he writes that perfect love will cast out all fear.

So many religious people are so afraid of so many things. I think our greatest fear is the fear of making a mistake and looking foolish. When we live in the fear of making a mistake the parameters of our lives become narrow. We never take a chance. We always try to stay safe. We will never be the first or the last to do something new and so we wallow in ecclesiastical mediocrity.

Living in the safe zone of life takes all passion and excitement out of our lives. We will never take a risk. We will never trust the impulses of the Holy Spirit in our prayers. We will never think in a creative and innovative fashion. We will always stick with the safe and the tried. The passing of the years will not bring wisdom or experience because all we do is the same thing in the same way year after year. Instead of moving ahead all we do is dig a rut that becomes deeper and deeper as the years go by.

Why are we afraid to take a chance? Why do we not trust ourselves, our gut, our Lord? Why are we always looking back and afraid to look ahead? Why are we so much more comfortable with tradition than with challenge?

Jesus tells us not to be afraid. Why do we still not trust that the one who died on the cross for us and gave us everything will take care of us? Why do we have so much trouble believing that the Holy Spirit dwells in us and will always show us the way if we but pay attention?

## The Healing of a Demon-Possessed Man

MARK 5:1-20

*Monday of the Fourth Week of the Year*

This gospel is frightening. The possessed Gerasene man strikes fear in our hearts and pity as well for the isolated life of insanity and violence that he lives. Breaking the fetters that bind him, screaming day and night in misery, and inflicting wounds on himself seem to be the lot—the life and death—of this poor soul. The demons tell Jesus plainly: "Legion is my name and there are hundreds of us!"

One of the most painful things that one can ever experience is to meet someone like this Gerasene. There are many of them. They are poor, tortured souls who never seem to have anything from life but pain, sorrow, and torture. They are people who live hopeless lives with no promise of any human comfort or love. Their hearts are broken by loneliness. There is no end to it all and no way out except the unthinkable—suicide. Many of our sisters and brothers live lives like this every day without exception.

Some of these poor sisters and brothers have been emotionally or physically abused. They were never able to grow into any real personhood or maturity. Others suffer the cross of mental illness and wander through life never really being able to be helped. Many are just rejected by family and society and left to live in the rocks like the poor outcast Gerasene. Some of our present day Gerasenes are people suffering from AIDS, drug addicts, people on death row, children forced into prostitution— the list goes on and on. And yes, there have been the times when you and I felt like the Gerasene and we didn't see a way out of our problems.

Jesus touched this poor soul. He wants to touch all the Gerasenes, but he can't do it without us. Jesus calls us to a discipleship of compassion and mercy for all the Gerasenes in our lives. Maybe just a kind word or a smile to a broken spirit can begin the process of casting out the demon. Perhaps as we recall our own camping-out times in the Gerasene territory on the "other side of the lake," we won't be so quick to judge and condemn another human being. Perhaps as we recall our own pain we can take another's hand and let them know that there is somebody who has been to the Gerasene territory and who understands. Perhaps in that moment of sharing our brokenness, poverty, and humanity, the process of healing can begin for another.

I believe that the Lord allows us our times in the Gerasene territory so that we will know what it's like to have nothing. Unfortunately, we forget so quickly and become cold and unfeeling. May the prayers of the Gerasene man in today's gospel keep us humble and human.

# Jairus' Daughter and the Sick Woman

## MARK 5:21-43

*Tuesday of the Fourth Week of the Year*

Today we read the beautiful accounts of the raising of Jairus' daughter and the healing of the woman afflicted with the hemorrhage for twelve years. In both accounts we are the witnesses of great faith in Jesus. Jairus and the woman believe with all their hearts that Jesus not only can, but will, help them.

Jesus tells the woman: "Daughter, it is faith that has cured you. Go in peace and be free of this illness," and to the officials at the news of Jairus' daughter's death: "Fear is useless. What is needed is trust."

When Jesus raises the little girl, he is the tender and compassionate healer and so sensitive to the love the parents have for their little girl. Their faith and love compel Jesus to act as he does. There is a power in their prayer that he cannot ignore.

When Jesus allows the touch of the sick woman to be the cause of her healing, he responds to the deep and bold faith on the part of this woman. She had more faith than did Jesus' disciples. "If I can touch his clothing I will get well."

Jairus and the woman are wonderful role models for the prayer of healing in the church today. All too frequently, our prayers for healing are sterile and "pro forma." We pray for, with, and over people, but we really don't expect, let alone demand, anything to happen. Our rituals become at times the celebration of a dying church that doesn't believe at all in the surprises of the Holy Spirit. We relegate healing to a sideshow type of evangelistic excess. How sad for the church.

Jesus will not heal unless, and until, *we* believe that he *can* heal and *wants* to heal. Jesus will not heal until *we* are passionately demanding it of God in the name of Jesus.

"Ask anything in my name!" The rebirth of the healing ministry will coincide with the rebirth of faith in the church. This faith has to be bold, daring, reckless, passionate, and sincere. In the parts of the body of Christ where one encounters such faith, one encounters healing and signs and wonders. Jairus and the woman are very much alive and well. Will we bring their faith to our church?

## A Prophet Without Honor

MARK 6:1-6

*Wednesday of the Fourth Week of the Year*

When the crowds asked, "Isn't this Joseph's son?" they were not asking in admiration. Their question was not the joy of neighbors and family over the success and achievement of one of their own. Not at all! These questions really could be framed: "Where does he get off?" "Who does he think he is?" They weren't able to hear or understand what Jesus was saying as he preached in the synagogue of Nazareth.

It is true that one's own family and close friends can be the worst people for a minister to try to help. There can be a built-in device that makes one question what another might possibly have to say to me. I *know* him. I know his family. I know the skeletons in his closets. I know his weak points.

It's not so far-fetched to imagine neighbors who could never take seriously the man who made their table and chairs. He's the carpenter. Period. He's no better. In fact, let me tell you about my boy!

Our problem can be similar to that of the people of Nazareth. We know Jesus too well. We are too used to the gospel. Let's face it, when the gospel is read we can sometimes put ourselves out in space, not because we are disrespectful, but because, honestly, we know the story by heart. "What can that priest say that I have not heard before? I've heard it all."

All too frequently the priest or deacon will give the same old sermon he's given so many times in the past. Nothing in the gospel has excited or touched him. What we have too often in churches is a bored priest telling a boring story to a group of people who are quickly approaching rigor mortis—so deadly can the experience be.

But imagine what could have happened in Nazareth if the people listened and didn't write off Jesus because they knew him. Imagine what can happen in our parishes when priests let the scriptures touch their hearts. Imagine what can happen where there is real Holy Spirit preaching to people who are hungry to hear the word and can't get enough of the real thing!

There is no doubt that the winds of the Holy Spirit are blowing across the church. Who knows what we may do! Miracles of grace are happening when the church opens the book together and invites the Holy Spirit in. Renew, Home Retreats, Cursillo, Marriage Encounter, prayer groups, small Christian communities—the list goes on and on of Pentecost happening all over the place.

What happened in Nazareth to Jesus so long ago must not happen in our communities. It will not if we all allow the Holy Spirit to open our hearts and speak to us.

## Sending Out the Twelve

### MARK 6:7-13

*Thursday of the Fourth Week of the Year*

Jesus sends the disciples out two-by-two. They have few earthly goods. They take nothing but a walking stick—no food, no traveling bag, not a coin in their

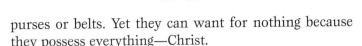

purses or belts. Yet they can want for nothing because they possess everything—Christ.

Reading this passage tends to make us a bit uncomfortable because Jesus is back to one of his favorite topics—poverty. The use of money and things continues to be a source of unending self-examination for the honest Christian. There's one thing for sure—from the Vatican to our own local parish, there is definitely no poverty! We all have more than we can ever use. Our lifestyles are definitely not like that of Jesus who has no place to lay his head.

There is a corollary that I think is worth considering: "The less of Jesus we possess the more of the world we need." We are almost completely an institutional church. The presence of the church is felt primarily in terms of buildings, programs, and material possessions. This materialistic church often drowns out the spiritual, and only in limited cases is the holy able to be experienced.

Would the poverty of this gospel solve our problems? I don't think so. I think we have to look at what the disciples *did* have as they went out to preach. First of all, they had community. They went out two-by-two. There was a reliance on and need for each other. A church has to be a community brought together by love, or it is nothing.

The disciples had the love of Christ in their hearts. Christ was their life. Christ was the meaning of all they were and all they did.

If Christ is really at the heart of our personal lives and at the heart of the church, then we will know how to use and enjoy the gifts of God, not as ends in themselves, but as ways of praising and glorifying God. When everything is experienced as a gift of our loving God, we learn to use each gift in a spirit of humble gratitude. We see all things as ways of praising God and serving our neighbor, especially the poor.

As we look into our own hearts, we know that the more we seek after, need, and abuse material things, the more we are losing hold of the greatest of all possessions—the love of Christ. We must seek him with all our hearts and know that he is always there for us, just for the asking. When we possess him we will know how to use the material blessings he gives us.

## The Death of John the Baptist

MARK 6:14-29

*Friday of the Fourth Week of the Year*

This is such a troubling and sad gospel. The execution of John the Baptist is so brutal and so evil. Today, in a country where men and women are executed, the gospel reminds us of our ethic of life. We must not take the life of a holy prophet, or the life of a serial killer. They are both precious in God's sight. "Thou shalt not kill" shouts at us as we choose death over life in capital punishment, abortion, poverty, and war. Our consistent ethic of life calls us to reverence and respect the rights of every person. It calls us to justice.

Perhaps the saddest part of the gospel story is the relationship between Herodias and her daughter. The mother encourages her daughter to do an erotic dance for Herod and his drinking buddies. So little has changed from then to now. What a heartbreak it is when a parent leads a child astray and is not the parent they should be for their children. And then comes the sin beyond all sins: "Ask for the head of John the Baptist." And she does. There are few moments in the whole of the Bible worse than this one. The story of Herodias rivals even that of David in his lust for Bathsheba that leads him to murder.

In the midst of this scene is Herod. Herod knew that John was a holy prophet. He was attracted by his words. If John had gotten through to him, he might have had a different place in history.

Herod is so taken by the sensuous Salome that with the several drinks under his belt he promises her under oath, "I'll give you anything you want, just ask me." His buddies are delighted. After spiritual direction from mom, Salome makes her request: "I want you to give me, at once, the head of John the Baptist on a platter." She gets her request and gives it to her mother: "Happy Mother's Day!"

Poor Herod, he really doesn't want to do this. Even he knows how evil this is. But the old demon of ego gets to him. "What will the boys think if I renege?" I wonder if Herod ever slept again. I wonder how much wine he had to consume each day to forget, at least for a while, his terrible sin.

Herod is a lot like us. He knows what is right, but he can't do it. He has sold out in so many ways that when the great test comes along he is powerless. Perhaps as we try to find meaning in the Herod story we might look at our own story. If we say "no" to the Lord in many little ways but promise to be faithful in the big things, we deceive ourselves. Virtue is not doing the big things for God, but rather doing the little things daily. Each day we have the opportunity to say "yes" to the Lord in so many ways. Let's not miss a single opportunity.

## The Return of the Twelve

MARK 6:30-34

*Saturday of the Fourth Week of the Year*

As the apostles return to Jesus from their evangelizing they are greeted by their loving teacher who invites them to come away with him and rest. Yes, the shepherds need to be shepherded. They need to rest and play. Jesus loves his friends so much and looks to their needs.

The rhythm of work, rest, and prayer is such a balanced one. Jesus is so holistic. He knows we need to be re-created. The life of the disciple must be punctuated with time for prayer, rest, and play.

No matter what our vocation—parent, religious, single person, etc.—we need time by ourselves to be re-created so that we will have something worthwhile to give our family or our flock.

So many people today are hungering for a prayer life. They know they need a space in their lives where they can find God. This search for God is not meant to be an escape from work and responsibilities. Rather, it is meant to empower us to return to our work and ministry with new enthusiasm and new power.

When we learn to pray each day our whole life is kept in balance. We learn what is important and what is not. We learn how to relate to people, how to love, and how to forgive. With Jesus leading and teaching us, all of our life becomes different and we deeply experience his beautiful peace.

Jesus so wants to lead us to the quiet place in our hearts, the place of silence. He wants to speak to us gently and lovingly. He won't shout at us. He invites and calls us and wants us to respond. The benefits of this kind of quiet and loving relationship in prayer are so great that our lives and everything in them are changed when we heed his invitation and prayer.

The One who loves us most speaks the words of life and hope that we yearn to hear. His love knows no limits. He is waiting to share more and more of it with us if we will only just invite him to enter that chamber of our heart that no one may enter unless we bid them welcome.

# Healing the Sick in Gennesaret

MARK 6:53-56

*Monday of the Fifth Week of the Year*

How much the people wanted to touch Jesus! Today's brief gospel tells the story of more and more of the sick and broken seeking after Jesus and not being satisfied until they could touch him. The gospel says that all who touched him got well. What does that mean?

I don't think it means that every leper who touched Jesus was healed or that every blind person who touched him could see. It does mean for them, as it does for us now, that everyone who touches Jesus in faith and love will be healed in *some* wonderful way.

When I come to Jesus in my own personal brokenness and beg for help, the very coming to Jesus with faith and love is healing for me. To come to Jesus in this way is to reach a point in my journey in which I am totally convinced of his love for me. I truly believe in the love Jesus has for me. I believe that he died on the cross for me. I believe that I am cherished and loved by the Son of God.

As I allow Jesus into the wounds of my heart, I allow him to be Lord of all of my life, dreams, hopes, joys, and failures. As I beg for the healing of a part of my heart, I first give to Jesus that part of my heart that is wounded. My simple prayer of handing over to Jesus my struggles and my agonies is the beginning of the healing process.

What is healing? It is more than sight restored, the disappearance of the cancer or addiction. Healing is making that part of my broken body or spirit a gift of Jesus. Healing is knowing and believing that I am precious to him even with my imperfections. Healing is knowing that he loves me and will never abandon me.

As one prays for healing, one is actually praying the prayer of complete abandonment to the will of God. One is praying for the Kingdom of God to be established in one's heart. There is too little prayer in the church for real healing, possibly because the results of such prayer change us forever.

## The Tradition of the Elders

MARK 7:1-13

*Tuesday of the Fifth Week of the Year*

This gospel, along with tomorrow's, is the Declaration of Independence for the followers of Jesus. Jesus has begun the revolution that is still being fought in today's church. Jesus is telling us once and for all that his religion isn't a religion at all, but is rather a way of living according to the call of God that flows from our hearts. We are authentic not when we follow some exterior laws (especially the man-made variety), but when our actions and thoughts and attitudes flow from the authenticity that we have achieved through faith and our own personal relationship with Jesus.

The Pharisees of yesterday, as well as the Pharisees of today, are frightened by what Jesus might do to the synagogue and to the present-day church. Make no mistake about it, Jesus is out to undermine and destroy all the sacred cows of the institutional church and all the sacred cows that we love because they protect us from taking him seriously.

It is very easy to take aim at the institution. We can all find laws, usages, traditions—sacred cows that have little to do with Jesus. But what about our own personal sacred cows? How many areas of our life have we declared "Corban"—dedicated to God—so that we are excused from our responsibilities? Frequently, keeping the law will get us out of doing what we know we should really do. Many people know they should be giving more time, interest, and attention to their spouse, children, or parents, yet they find ways to get around it! "I'm so busy." "I'm so stressed out." "I just don't have the time"—we are all masters at making excuses for not giving the gift our families so need from us—our time and our love.

Many have created a materialistic lifestyle to serve the people they love the most but lose their loved ones in the process. How many couples and families will practically kill themselves working to have a week in the Islands and discover that they are vacationing with strangers!

I hate this gospel. It cuts through many shallow attempts to create my own religion, to serve my own needs rather than to listen to the voice of Jesus and to follow it.

What are your sacred cows? How is Jesus calling you to authentic religion?

## Clean and Unclean

MARK 7:14-23

*Wednesday of the Fifth Week of the Year*

Jesus continues to pull away all the foundations of the religion of his people. Now he does away with "Kosher"—clean and unclean foods—and teaches a profound lesson in the process.

Holiness comes from our hearts; evil also comes from our hearts. Jesus was taking away from his listeners a very comfortable crutch. "If I eat the right food, if I fast, if I keep the rules, if I go to church on Sunday, then I'm holy." How easy it would be if that were the case!

Unfortunately, it's much harder. We are holy by how we think, live, and treat others. Our holiness is not just conditioned on following a daily rule book, but on what we do each day to ourselves and to other people.

Externals can be wonderful. Fasting, prayer schedules, etc., are all very helpful after we have first established and accepted a personal and loving relationship with Jesus in which all the parts of our hearts are open to the touch and to the rule of the Good Shepherd. We realize then that the externals have no power in themselves, but only as they express and celebrate the interior relationships we have with the Lord.

Holiness consists in knowing and loving Jesus Christ in a completely open and honest manner in which every part of us is given to him and we hold back nothing for ourselves. This process of acquiring the mind and heart of Jesus takes a lifetime. But when we are honest in the process, when we truly seek him, then it is much more likely that what will come from our hearts is love and peace, tenderness and compassion.

## The Faith of the Syrophoenician Woman

MARK 7:24-30

*Thursday of the Fifth Week of the Year*

There's no question that today's meeting of Jesus and the Syrophoenician woman was a growth experience. This Gentile lady is a mother who obviously adores her daughter. She'll do anything for her daughter's healing, even go through the humiliation of begging this Jewish rabbi to come and heal her.

Jesus is trying to "hide out" in a house in the territory of Tyre and Sidon. He's probably exhausted from his entanglements with the Pharisees. He wants to be left alone. This woman, not even a Jew, seeks him out. Does she believe in him? Probably not. Does Jesus know she doesn't believe in him? Probably. Does it annoy him that she doesn't believe but is still looking for a favor? Absolutely!

Jesus states the obvious: he has come first for the Jewish people. Jesus refers to them as the children and says that the bread is for the children, not the dogs. This incredible woman proceeds to put Jesus in his place as no one ever has or ever will again. Can you imagine the tone of voice of this woman who has just heard her daughter referred to as a dog!

Her response is not a sweet, self-effacing, and humble request of a poor soul. It is a gutsy, proud, and beautiful put-down of the One who should have known better, using his own image of the dogs licking up the crumbs.

"For such a reply, be off now! The demon has already left your daughter!" Jesus tells her. There's no "faith has cured her" stuff here. This great lady replies like a woman, a mother. She replies from a source of power and love as old as humanity. She speaks as a mother who loves her child more than life itself.

Jesus learned some lessons that day. The first lesson was that he had to learn to bend a few of his own rules about who is first and second in the Kingdom. The second lesson was that there is nothing on this earth as powerful as the love of a mother for a child and that a mother will do anything to save her child, even endure the sarcasm of a tired and worn out rabbi. The third lesson is that courtesy and manners sometimes mean more than being right or even divine.

## Jesus Heals a Deaf Man

MARK 7:31-37

*Friday of the Fifth Week of the Year*

I was privileged to hear this marvelous gospel about speaking and hearing at the Benedictine Abbey of Glastonbury. It seemed so appropriate to hear the gospel in this wonderful place where so much attention is paid to listening and to speaking.

Hours of the day are spent in the chapel where the psalms, hymns, the scriptures, and prayers are spoken. They are spoken and sung with deep faith and simplicity as a tradition more than 1500 years old is fulfilled each day from before the sun's rising to the dark of another night. Everything in the monk's day and activity is expressed in the holy moment when he sings the praises of God at Office.

The monk does more than speak; he listens. He is constantly being formed by the power of the word at Office and at *lectio divina. Lectio divina* ("holy listening") is the attentive listening with our whole being to the scriptures, the living word of God. Whether the Lectio is communal or private, the monk is totally present to the word. That word, sharper than any two-edged sword, pierces and transforms the monk's heart. In Lectio, he pauses as a word, an image, a feeling, or a thought touches him and leads him to prayer and a response.

As Christians we need so much to be still so that we can listen. We listen so that we will have something to say. Today, as Jesus cures the deaf man with the speech impediment, we think of the ritual within the celebration of baptism in which the Lord is asked to open the ears of the child so that he or she may be able to hear the word.

We pray that the Lord will open our ears so that we can hear him speak. Our Lord speaks softly. We must consciously drown out the noise around us to enter into our inner heart and go deeper into God's love if we are really to hear God's voice. God is *always* speaking to us. God speaks in the word, in people, in the events and experiences of our lives. Our job is not to get the Lord to speak, but to be quiet enough to hear and feel him speaking to us. He is always speaking! Listening to him speak is a prayer.

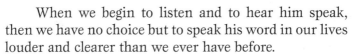

When we begin to listen and to hear him speak, then we have no choice but to speak his word in our lives louder and clearer than we ever have before.

But, we cannot listen unless we are first silent. The developing of a prayer life begins only when we are no longer afraid of being silent and alone with God.

## The Feeding of the Four Thousand

MARK 8:1-10

*Saturday of the Fifth Week of the Year*

Jesus is moved with pity for the hungry crowd. We know that as sensitive as he was to their physical hunger, he was even more aware of their spiritual and emotional hunger. Feeding the hunger of men and women is really what the ministry of Jesus is all about. He feeds the hungry, comforts the fearful, and touches the brokenhearted. All of Christian ministry comes down to feeding and healing the needs of our neighbor as we allow them to feed and heal our souls.

The scene of the multiplication of the loaves and the fishes is a prelude to the eucharist. The eucharist is for people who are hungry and yearning for God's mercy. The people gathered around Jesus on this day and at every Mass that is ever celebrated are the poor, the broken, the sinners, and the sick—all of us. We come to eucharist not from a position of power, but from one of weakness and brokenness. We come to eat and drink because we will collapse on the journey without Jesus and his life-giving food.

This eucharist is not the food of angels; it is the food for sinners. It is the sustenance of normal men and women trying to follow Jesus but struggling and falling often along the way. It is the food of sinners so aware that they are not worthy and that everything is grace and gift. We pray the prayer with such understanding: "O

Lord, I am not worthy . . . but only say the word and I shall be healed."

We have nothing to give to Jesus—only seven loaves of bread and a few small fishes. What is that among so many? Nothing! What do I have to give to Jesus? Just my failures, broken promises, disappointment, and infidelities. What can they accomplish? Nothing.

But if, like the seven loaves and the fish, we place what we are in the hands of Jesus, he will work miracles. He will feed the multitudes. He will bring grace, mercy, healing, and love to so many if we just place the little we have in his hands and try not to do it ourselves. We may think what we have to place in the hands of Jesus is nothing, but he doesn't!

## The Demand for a Sign

MARK 8:11-13

*Monday of the Sixth Week of the Year*

The Pharisees want proof! They demand a sign from Jesus to prove that he is the prophet and to justify the leap of faith required of them to become his disciples. Can you blame them? Can you blame us? They, and we, want a sure thing. We never get a sure thing. We are all forced to leap with no net to catch us. We are all forced to be with him or against him. There really is no other way.

Jesus would have loved a sign, a sure thing on the cross. Did he know that his death would end in resurrection? Did he know that there would be a happy ending? No. He did not. He was forced to leap out in faith and give the Father everything. That was what the Father demanded, and Jesus gave no less.

We want a sign so often. We want a sure thing. "Will my marriage work out? Is this decision correct? Am I really doing God's will? Should I be a priest?

Should we have another child? Should I give my spouse another chance? Is it time to try once more or to divorce?" These are all very hard questions. How much easier it would be if the Lord would give us a sign, a sure thing so that we could know what he wants of us!

But Jesus is the sign. Jesus is the sure thing. If the Pharisees had really listened to Jesus, they would have come to know that *he* was the sign. He was the truth. He was the presence of God's love among us. One can never know who Jesus is if one remains a casual observer. We know the truth and we can tell what the sign is when we have allowed ourselves to listen and to respond to Jesus a step at a time, a day at a time.

The Pharisees want an external proof—a sign of who and what Jesus is. All that is possible is the internal certitude one can come to by knowing and responding to the call of Jesus, day by day. The Pharisees wanted career guarantee, and all that Jesus will give us is the internal security that comes from the growth of love.

Henri Nouwen, the great spiritual writer, was fascinated by the trapeze family, the Flying Wallendas. Part of that fascination was the faith of the acrobat who let go of his or her swing and plunged into mid-air only to be caught in mid-air by another acrobat. Isn't faith like that: letting go in mid-air and believing the Lord will catch us?

## The Yeast of the Pharisees and Herod

MARK 8:14-21

*Tuesday of the Sixth Week of the Year*

Communication is not always easy, not even for Jesus and the disciples. The word "yeast" for both parties means something entirely different. The disciples are thinking in terms of the material, in terms of bread, while Jesus is using the term to mean the evil qualities of the Pharisees and Herod against which they should be on guard.

It seems to us to be an understandable mistake for the disciples. We probably would have made it ourselves. But Jesus seems to be very upset by it. I wonder why?

Perhaps Jesus has been trying to raise gradually the sights and understanding of the disciples to a higher and more spiritual way of looking at things. After all, Jesus has been their teacher and mentor. He has been revealing to them all that is in his heart. He has been trying to lead them to a deeper maturity and understanding.

They, like us, slip back to the old ways all too easily. In a very profound moment of trying to teach them about the forces of evil and the power of personal compromise, they think only of their stomachs and are worried that they forget to bring bread—as if the one who multiplied the loaves twice would allow them to go hungry.

The disciples will forget on many occasions all that Jesus had tried to teach them. They will forget about the meaning of humility and service as they struggle for a higher position in the Kingdom. They will deny the need for the cross and the sufferings of the Messiah. The will constantly see the work of Jesus in terms of political power rather than loving service. The disciples are a slow lot, and so are we.

But Jesus never gives up on them or on us. He loves them and us so much. He is so patient with them and with us. Jesus begins all over again as the good Rabbi who doesn't stop teaching. He continues to share his love, his heart, and his dream until that day when it finally clicks with them and with us. The Good Shepherd is so patient.

Perhaps we have to learn patience. It takes a long time to become human. It takes a long time to become a man or woman of faith. Each day we begin all over again. Each day we pick up the Book to find him. Each day we go to work to try to find his face among those with whom

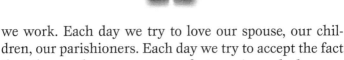

we work. Each day we try to love our spouse, our children, our parishioners. Each day we try to accept the fact that they and we are not perfect—we're only human. Thank you, God, for being so patient with us!

## The Blind Man of Bethsaida

MARK 8:22-26

*Wednesday of the Sixth Week of the Year*

In this beautiful gospel of the healing of the blind man, Jesus does something to him that is so touching and tender; he takes the man's hand and leads him outside the village and cures him.

How safe this man must have felt with his hand in Jesus' hand. Jesus leads him, and he has nothing to fear, for the warmth and firmness of the Lord's hand reassures this man that all is well.

When we are blind and lost, when we are afraid and confused, Jesus is there to take our hand and to lead us to safety. Why is it that we can believe in the healing love of Jesus for other people, but when it comes to ourselves we are awkward and afraid to let Jesus take our hand?

Sometimes we act like rugged individualists and think there's something unseemly or weak about praying for our own needs, including healing. We're there for other people. We pray over the sick and troubled as we remind Jesus how much he loves his people and how much he wants to heal his people. We claim the victory of Jesus for other people, but we are very shy in asking for ourselves.

Let's pray about Jesus taking our hand and leading us to safety. Let's picture him taking us to safety and leading us out of the turmoil and fear that we face. Let's allow him to lead us home where we will be safe with him and where his love will be our healing.

It takes a lot of faith and humility to pray for personal healing. It requires a real letting go and placing ourselves in his protection. We must walk where he wishes us to go. We sometimes have to experience some bizarre signs and wonders like resting in the spirit or having Jesus use spittle for healing.

Maybe personal healing demands that we have to abdicate some personal control and power and place ourselves in his loving hands without knowing where we are going or how we will get there. To beg for any kind of healing is to place ourselves totally defenseless in his hands and just believe that he will take care of us.

And yes, sometimes it takes spittle to do it. We want instantaneous healing. Most often, that's not how it comes. It comes through spittle, and pain, and patience. But it does come the way we need it most. The blind man was so glad he took the hand of Jesus and so glad he let Jesus lead him, and so will we be.

## Peter's Declaration About Jesus

MARK 8:27-33

*Thursday of the Sixth Week of the Year*

"Who do people say that I am?" With that question Jesus begins the newest phase of his formation of the disciples. He will draw out of them the answers to the two major questions of life: identity and destiny.

The first part of the questioning is easy. It's no great thing to tell Jesus what other people are saying about him. Their responses are probably what they think Jesus wants to hear: John the Baptist, Elijah, one of the prophets—not bad company to be part of! But then Jesus turns the table and invites Peter into a personal response and commitment—"Who do *you* say that I am?" Peter rises to the occasion: "You are the Messiah!"

Each of us must come to the moment of profession of our own personal faith in Jesus. We reach a point where the faith of others no longer suffices. It is no longer meaningful to process the faith of our parents or priests or teachers. We must come to that holy time when we no longer profess other people's faith or liturgical creeds, but we must stand and speak on our own and profess: "I believe."

When we reach that moment of personal faith, we are never the same again and our faith is never the same. We have entered into a new way of believing and being.

When the church and the catechumens prepare each Lent for the renewal of the baptismal promises at Easter Mass, the hope of the church is that it will not be a "pro forma" liturgical nicety, but that we will really profess our faith in the risen Lord.

All that we are doing now is to prepare our hearts to respond and to say our "yes," especially with our reading and praying on the word of God. It all is meant to help us to come to a deeper moment of faith and love in the Lord. We have been invited to mature and deepen our faith and come to know that we, too, are the body of Christ and that his life is our life.

Faith is a very lonely place. It is the place where we are alone with the living God. He holds our hands in his, and there is no one but the Lord and ourselves. He looks into our eyes and says, "Do you believe?" Our response determines everything in life.

For we come to understand that our identity is to be Christ, and our destiny is to share in his destiny—the laying down of our lives in loving service as he laid down his on the cross.

Let Jesus take your hands in his, look into his eyes, and answer his question: "Do you believe?"

# The Cost of Discipleship

*Friday of the Sixth Week of the Year*

Jesus continues to teach us about who we are (our identity) and what we must be about (our destiny). Our life choices flow from our understanding of who we are as a member of Christ's body.

It is very consoling, warm, and rewarding to know and possess the Lord Jesus and his love. Living out the relationship is another question. Discipleship costs. The cost is the giving of our very selves to Jesus and to the community.

Jesus says it as it is: "If a person wishes to come after me, they must deny their very self, take up their cross and follow me. Whoever would save their life must lose it. What does it profit, . . ." etc. The point is very clear, the disciple lives out the identity of being part of Christ by embracing the Paschal Mystery. It will only be in denying what is not of Jesus that we will find life.

The cross is part and parcel of all of our lives. There's no escaping it. It doesn't mean that we go out of our way to find it. Life will bring us so many opportunities in which we can embrace the cross in little ways and thus be born once again to a new life. We have so many opportunities to say the kind word when we are tempted to respond with the mean or sarcastic word. We are constantly invited to give a little bit more of ourselves to our dear families and friends. We are always being invited by the Lord to think of another's needs before our own. The Paschal Mystery which is the Lord's death and resurrection is happening in our life as we follow in the footsteps of Jesus.

Today's scripture invites us to look at our lives. Are we following in the loving and humble footsteps of Jesus, or are we following in another path in which our comfort and well-being is the prime concern rather than the care of our little flock?

"What does someone profit in gaining the whole world and losing their soul in the process?" These are very serious words Jesus speaks to us, and this is the time to ponder them and to respond by walking a bit closer to Jesus.

## The Transfiguration

MARK 9:2-13

*Saturday of the Sixth Week of the Year*

The transfiguration is an incredible moment for Peter, James, and John. They see the divinity of Jesus shine through the humanity. They know their friend Jesus is truly the Son of God. What an experience for them to see his glory. They will never forget it or be the same again.

It seems that each one of us needs a "transfiguration moment," a moment when we *know*, we don't just believe, but we *know* that Jesus Christ is the Son of God and that his love has brought us new life.

So much of what the church concerns itself with is intellectual knowledge of God. We catechize, teach, and evangelize people all through their lives. We presume that knowing the concepts is knowing the Person. It's not, not by a long shot.

The most effective tools for conversion in the church of Vatican II have been those experiences that have touched people's hearts. The church has worked hard to create different programs in which it becomes more possible for a Christian to really be touched by God and have a mystical experience. Think about it. If we have never really experienced God how can we ever pray? To what or to whom are we praying if we don't really know that God exists?

Thank God for the experience of directed retreats, Marriage Encounter, Cursillo, Life in the Spirit seminars, Baptism in the Holy Spirit, Renew 2000, Antioch weekends, etc. There have been so many beautiful and touching moments in which people have met their God. Hopefully, spirit-filled Sunday liturgies can also achieve this.

Have you had your transfiguration experience? Is the experience of God's love and power still fresh in your mind and in your heart? If not, why not speak to someone about how you, too, can experience the power of the Holy Spirit and go up the mountain to be present at the transfiguration. Effort is required to have the transfiguration experience. You must climb the mountain. That climbing may mean going on the Marriage Encounter, directed retreat, or making a Life in the Spirit seminar leading to baptism in the Holy Spirit.

Once you have experienced the power of God in this way nothing is ever the same again. The eucharist, the sacraments, and the scriptures take on a whole new meaning and dimension. God is truly alive. You deserve to be present at the transfiguration. Start your climb to the top of the mountain. Demand of the Lord the gift of experiencing his presence and his love. Give him the space and the time for it to happen and it will!

## The Healing of a Boy With a Demon

MARK 9:14-29

*Monday of the Seventh Week of the Year*

In this scene of the curing of the boy possessed by the mute demon, we are shocked by the severity of the evil one's possession of the boy but moved by the loving care and fidelity of the father. The father's only concern is the well-being of his beloved son. He will do anything to help the boy, even to bring him to the good rabbi to see if he can do anything to help.

In their conversation, Jesus calls the father to something he never bargained for that day. Jesus calls him to faith and new life. Jesus responds sharply to the father's plea: "If you *can*!" He gives the father the challenge of his life: "Everything is possible to the one who believes." The father then expresses his, and our, constant struggle and dilemma—we do and we don't believe. The father asks Jesus to help his unbelief. What a precious moment that is in this man's life, and in our own life! When we can honestly tell Jesus that our faith is conditional, that it's not perfect, that we are struggling, then we give the Lord the greatest and most beautiful gift of all. We give him ourselves just as we are!

That gift to the Lord of our real self is all that has any value. When we give him ourselves, then we are saying to Jesus that *we* are not Savior—*he* is the Savior.

That gift of our true self to the Lord is the abdication of control and power on our part. It is the recognition that it is God's love that sustains us and brings us through every difficulty and struggle. This gift is the gift of the humble person who knows that in the hands of our loving Lord our weakness becomes strength, our poverty, riches, and our brokenness, wholeness.

"I do believe! Help my unbelief!" Jesus' word thunders forever in our hearts: "Mute and deaf spirit, I command you: Get out of him and never enter him again!" Jesus says these words of liberation over us as we come to him and give him our brokenness and our pain. We must be active. We cannot hide from him because we are not perfect. We come to him as we are and we give Jesus the gift that most delights him: the gift of a loving, broken, but sincere heart yearning for the healing touch of Jesus Christ.

# Who Is the Greatest?

MARK 9:30-37

*Tuesday of the Seventh Week of the Year*

When I pray about Jesus and his relationship with the disciples it gives me great reassurance that there's hope for me. This scene of the journey through Galilee is a wonderful example. Jesus is beginning to reveal to them the real purpose of his ministry of the Paschal Mystery as he unfolds the frightening but necessary fact that he will be delivered to the hands of sinners and will be put to death but rise from the dead.

The disciples reacted just as you might imagine: they ignored his words and dismissed them. They were frightened. After all, they weren't following Jesus to be part of a failure, but to be very successful. They had plans of doing good for people, but in the process they would also do well for themselves, their wives, and for their children. Jesus and his ministry were growing more successful each day. True, Jesus would go to extremes some days about giving one's life for another and poverty and things like that, but they could calm him down and make his teaching more "practical" and "real."

When you really come down to brass tacks, Jesus needed the disciples more than they needed him. Oh, they loved him and were devoted to him, at least for the most part, but they were also necessary, and they would be afforded the places of prestige, power, and financial reward that their position demanded. They would do much good for Jesus and certainly would return the accomplishment. That was only fair.

When they got home to Capernaum, Jesus asked them what they were discussing on the way home. They fell silent because they had been talking about nothing but their place and prestige in the new Kingdom. They were lusting for power, authority, position, recognition, and money—all the things that Jesus told them were not of the Kingdom.

Jesus didn't give up on them, as he doesn't with you or me. Patiently, he teaches them again that, in his new Kingdom, authority and power mean not being the one on top, but the lowest, the servant of all. Jesus will teach this lesson over and over. The washing of the feet at the Last Supper will be the most dramatic and moving of all of his attempts to teach them and us. He never gives up on us. Thank God!

## "Anyone Who Is Not Against Us Is With Us"

MARK 9:38-40

*Wednesday of the Seventh Week of the Year*

In this short gospel Jesus sets the guidelines and principles of ecumenical and interfaith dialogue. Jesus calls us to look beyond the boundaries of the tribe, the nation, religion, and common philosophy. He tells the disciples right out: "Anyone who is not against us is with us."

Our premise for so many years, even centuries, was that those who were not of our Catholic faith were enemies. How many sins against God's love were committed in the name of religion! When we look at our record of sins against the Jews, Protestants, Moslems, etc., the list is staggering. We, who were to be the preachers of the gospel of love, became content to luxuriate in sectarian isolation considering all others evil because they did not possess "the truth."

We almost never saw the good that others were doing or the truth and beauty that they were teaching and preaching. In reality, almost everything one hears in a church or synagogue is the message of God's love. Pope John XXIII and the Vatican Council called us to embrace one another, to talk to one another, to learn from one another, and to pray with one another.

How rich our church becomes when we are in loving and open dialogue with sisters and brothers of other faiths. We have so much to teach one another. Jesus calls us to tear down the walls that separate and divide us and to learn to live together in peace and mutual service.

It is the time and guidance of the Holy Spirit when, and if, the churches will become one organically and structurally. In the meantime, we have to live and act as if we were already one. We *are* one when we live in love and service to one another.

As we allow Jesus to melt away all vestiges of prejudice in our hearts, we see the Kingdom of God more powerfully in our lives and in our churches. As we begin to see everyone as friend and sister or brother, we know that Jesus is truly present and with us.

As true as this is in terms of ecumenical dialogue, how much more truthful it is in the internal life of Catholics themselves. We need to learn from, and talk to, one another.

## Temptations to Sin

MARK 9:41-50

*Thursday of the Seventh Week of the Year*

In this gospel Jesus tells us that if we give even just a cup of cold water to someone because he or she belongs to Christ, we will not go without a reward. He then proceeds to tell us of the punishment we will receive if we harm one of his little ones. Jesus is teaching us about the unity of his body. We all belong to him and to one another. To do good to the lowliest or to hurt the most humble is really to do good or evil to Jesus himself, and thus to deserve reward or punishment.

Jesus then proceeds to teach us a very difficult lesson: that we sometimes have to do violence to ourselves to free ourselves from something that is causing us great harm. While Jesus certainly doesn't advocate plucking our eyes out or amputating limbs, he does mean that there are things we must do to be whole that will cost and be painful.

Is there any pain equal to that of breaking off an illicit but loving relationship? Can anyone even begin to imagine that pain a man or woman undergoes when he or she tries to break off a relationship with someone who is already married or not free? Cutting off a limb might be easier. What about the hell a person goes through who is trying to kick a habit of drug abuse! Alcoholics who try to live a life of sobriety know the pain Jesus was referring to.

Perhaps our amputations aren't as severe as the ones mentioned, but whenever we are faced with the knowledge that we must change, if we are to be healthy, it means real pain and a kind of amputation. This pruning is part of the life of every sensitive Christian. It might be as harmless as knowing we should cut down on television viewing, go on a diet, stop smoking, start exercising, go to bed earlier, rise earlier, spend more time with our children or spouse, etc.

Whenever we know we have to change we know it will hurt, and that's why we resist it. It takes us back to Mark 9 and the challenge that Jesus gives us to be whole and healthy. Sometimes that can't happen without doing some real violence, but the pain is always worth the result—freedom.

# Marriage and Divorce

## MARK 10:1-12

*Friday of the Seventh Week of the Year*

Jesus teaches us today about the indissolubility of marriage. It is not an easy time for marriage and family. Our whole culture makes sport of fidelity while promiscuity and sexual freedom seem to be the virtues of the day. Many couples who come to marry in the church have been living together and come from divorced homes themselves. The "philosophy" they have heard from childhood, if not from their parents, then certainly from the media and their peers: "If it doesn't work out you can always get out of it."

The church has a sacred and holy responsibility to uphold marriage as the precious gift it is from God and to help its people prepare and celebrate marriage that will bring peace, joy, happiness, and healing to the whole church. It is God's plan for husband and wife to find meaning and purpose in the love they share. That love must be a daily decision. One must work at loving and make a daily commitment to allow that love to grow.

Many times a couple getting married will choose the Gospel of John, chapter 15, where Jesus tells them to love one another as he loved them first.

Symbolically, the couple pronounces their vows beneath the crucifix. It is so fitting because the love of Jesus for his beloved spouse, the church, is the model of how the couple must love each other.

Married love is the free gift of one's life and being to the beloved. One lays down his or her life for the beloved. Each day is another opportunity to decide to love. Every action of the day is an act of love—from driving to work, to mowing the lawn, to lovemaking. It is all part of the gift of self to the beloved.

The love of the couple is an experience of God. We are speaking of such a holy and sacred mystery when we speak of this great sacrament of marriage.

The church must do everything possible to help affirm and learn from the mystery of marriage. Pre-Cana programs, Marriage Enrichment, Marriage Encounter, Retrouvaille, Marriage and Family Life programs—all of these are the sacred responsibility of the church to help her people cherish and live this holy sacrament.

The other responsibility of the church is to reach out to, love, embrace, and affirm all those who are not married or whose marriages end. Each Sunday as I celebrate mass I look out at so many beautiful and holy sisters and brothers who are single parents. They are working so hard at being the best parents they can be. There are so many divorced, separated, and remarried parishioners who are there just like everyone else looking to be nourished by the word and trying to give their children a faith in Jesus.

God forbid that we ever be unwelcoming or judgmental or cold to these holy ones who are our modern day saints struggling so hard to put the pieces of their lives back together and to find God's love and a place in the church.

While the church is still groping and struggling to find a way for official reconciliation for our divorced sisters and brothers, let them find nothing but the embrace of loving welcome in our parishes where everyone belongs and everyone has a place at the table.

Let us pray for our church that is trying to be faithful to the law. Perhaps we, too, will be able to incorporate the pastoral gentleness and understanding that the eastern churches practice into our own pastoral practice.

# Jesus and the Little Children

## MARK 10:13-16

*Saturday of the Seventh Week of the Year*

Today's gospel presents us with the beautiful picture of Jesus and the children. How he loves them and how they love him. It is an absolute, iron-clad rule that the more a parish loves, cherishes, and works for its children, the more successful and blessed the parish will be. It is true. Why is it true? Because when parents see that the church loves their children they know that the church is reaching out to them and loving them too.

We believe that each child is the Christ Child born to us again and present in our lives. When a couple brings their child to baptism, they are inviting Jesus into the life of their child and their lives too. To love a child and to raise a child is the holiest thing a person can ever do. I believe that every loving father and mother has to go straight to heaven when they die because they have done the most important and the holiest thing a person can do: they have brought Christ into the world and formed this child truly to be another Jesus.

The call to holiness that God gives a mother and father is very direct. He calls them to love their child and to lay down their lives each day in love for each other and their children. *That* is their sanctity—loving with all they have and all they are. The sanctity of the couple raising a family does not consist of spending huge amount of times at church or formal prayer. Their prayer is the daily loving and giving. That is marriage and parenthood.

When the community comes together on Sunday, the church's responsibility is to remind the parents of what they already possess—*everything*—and to encourage and challenge them to live out the commitments they made in the holy vows and in parenthood. The church cannot give its people holiness—they already have it. What the church does is very important—it reminds couples of who they are and what they possess, and it inspires and challenges them to live it.

The gospel ends with Jesus embracing, blessing, and placing his hands upon these children when parents hold and love their little ones and when the church reaches out to hold and love and cherish our beloved children. There is nothing more important, nothing more beautiful, nothing holier than to hold and love, care for and protect all of God's children. That's what Jesus did. When his church does it, it can't go wrong.

## The Rich Young Man

MARK 10:17-27

*Monday of the Eighth Week of the Year*

Get ready for some good guilt. First of all, anyone who is able to read this book in a nice warm house, with a tummy full of food is part of the group that Jesus was referring to when he used the term "rich."

The rich young man is you and I. There's no doubt about it. We are among the richest people who have ever lived in the history of the human race. Compared to most of the people Jesus knew, and compared to the vast majority of the inhabitants of planet Earth, we live like royalty.

We are also good, moral people, again, just like the rich young man. He asks what he must do to share everlasting life. Jesus responds by stating the Ten Commandments. The young man says that he has done all these things since his childhood. Looking on him with love, Jesus drops the bomb: "Go and sell what you have and give it to the poor . . . after that, come and follow me." The gospel tells us, "His face fell and he went away sad, for he had many possessions."

71

Jesus goes on to explain the dangers of riches and possessions and how they keep us from the Kingdom.

What do we do with this gospel? The church has softened it over the years by saying that Jesus was advocating the "spirit" of poverty, not absolute poverty. St. Francis thought that Jesus meant it literally. Obviously, very few other Christians did, or do, take it too literally. Luke's beatitude is "Blessed are the poor." The church softened Matthew's to, "Blessed are the poor in spirit."

To me, this is one of those moments when the whole church (with a few Mother Teresa/Dorothy Day type exceptions) has to confess that we are sinners and are not, or maybe even cannot, live up to Jesus' call to follow him as his true disciple.

Let us not walk away. Where would we go? At least we know we have a Jesus who loves us even in our imperfections and sinfulness. Even though we can't reach one hundred percent in following the letter of what he calls for, we can live the spirit of Jesus in simplicity and try to have a heart-filled desire to share what we have with the poor.

## Following Jesus

MARK 10:28-31

*Tuesday of the Eighth Week of the Year*

We see a very tender Jesus responding to the plea of Peter: "We have put aside everything to follow you!" Jesus responds by promising Peter that he will receive a hundred times more than the wonderful things they have left.

Make no mistake about it, Peter and the others left a lot of things to follow Jesus. His fishing business was his pride and joy. Probably his cousins and friends took over, but he was still away from it and he missed it. He knew that no one could run it like he could. But Jesus said: "Come, follow me!"

Peter left behind his house and his family. He might go days, even weeks at a time, not seeing his wife and children, and he missed them so much. There were the money problems that his absence created as he took less of the profit because of the extra hands filling in for him. But Jesus said: "Come, follow me."

Peter didn't even appreciate yet what discipleship would eventually cost him—his very life. The cost of discipleship is always high. As we see what it cost the martyrs of El Salvador, we realize that Jesus demands a lot from those who would be his disciples—he demands everything.

Jesus says to each of us: "Come, follow me." We are all asked to give up a lot if we want to walk with the Lord. In all vocations the great command is to love the way Jesus loved. When we love our spouses, children, friends, and parishioners in that way we give up so much of our own will, selfishness, egoism, and prejudice. When our life is lived like Jesus' life—giving ourselves to others—the cost is high, but the rewards are beyond our wildest dreams.

A hundredfold is nothing to what Jesus gives to those who love him and his little ones. Our joy and reward is beyond our imagining. The God of mercy and generosity gives us the grace to make any sacrifice we must. He is always with us. His reward is possessing Love himself—forever.

Jesus said: "Come, follow me."

# The Request of James and John

## MARK 10:32-45

*Wednesday of the Eighth Week of the Year*

"Can you drink the cup?" This is the question Jesus asked the sons of Zebedee, James and John (after a long teaching on the meaning of discipleship, poverty, and the cost of following him), to which they responded, "See to it that we sit at your right and left when you come into your glory."

They ask for this favor right after the prediction of his passion and death that Jesus had just made to the disciples. They obviously didn't have a clue as to what Jesus was talking about. Let's not feel so bad that it takes us so long!

One of Henri Nouwen's last books was *Can You Drink the Cup?* It is a moving book of how he matured as a man and as a priest through more than thirty-five years of priesthood. Henri drank the blood of Christ for the first time from his priest uncle's golden chalice. When the golden chalice quickly changed into clay and glass and lesser materials, Henri began to realize the meaning of drinking from the Lord's cup. It was not glory but sacrificial gift. Drinking from his cup meant to be one with him as he lays down his life in loving sacrifice for humanity. It means sharing the pain of the sick, the lonely, the unloved, the alienated, the prisoner, the addict, and the despised. Each Christian is asked as James and John were, "Can you drink this cup?"

As we say we will drink it, we give our lives to Jesus and to one another. As we say these words, we take upon ourselves the hopes, joys, dreams, and pains of the family. We never again live alone for ourselves. We live with the family as they become "bone of our bone" and "flesh of our flesh."

Like James and John, Henri and we take a long time to understand the meaning of the cup. We pick it up and the Lord's gentle grace helps it. He sustains us in our doubts and failures. He holds us in our weakness. Yes, we can drink the cup because Jesus helps us every inch of the way.

## Blind Bartimaeus

MARK 10:46-52

*Thursday of the Eighth Week of the Year*

"Jesus, Son of David, have pity on me!" This prayer bursting from the heart of Bartimaeus is the famous Jesus Prayer. It is prayed unceasingly all over the earth. It is perhaps the most meaningful and powerful prayer ever prayed. I ask you to please read my reflection on Luke's version of the scene found on the Monday of the Thirty-Third Week of the Year. I would like, however, to comment on the conclusion of today's gospel.

The gospel says: "Immediately he received his sight and started to follow Jesus up the road." What a great end to such a powerful story of faith! But actually, it's a beginning, not an ending. It's the beginning of a new life for Bartimaeus as he goes from darkness to light, from despair to joy. It is the beginning of his new life—to follow Jesus up the road where he goes.

If we read the accounts of the healing miracles in the gospels, we will notice that there is always a string attached to the gift. Jesus gives the cured person a job after he or she receives healing. The healed person is called upon to become a healer and to continue what Jesus began in his or her life. Healing or forgiveness is never meant to be just a private or personal gift. It is always meant to be something given to the whole community. As Bartimaeus follows Jesus up the road, he is filled with the joy and excitement of helping others to see Jesus and learn about him.

Think of all the times Jesus has touched us with forgiveness, healing, mercy, or reconciliation. What a grace it is to feel his touch. He brings life and love where there had previously been death and despair. We get a new lease on life. We begin again. But that's not good enough.

Do we have the sense of responsibility to share the gift with another? Do we become the sacrament of healing or forgiveness for a sister or brother who can only know the touch of Jesus through our touch? We belong with Jesus—following him up the road to meet the crowd along the way that is waiting for us to bring them his gentle touch.

## Cleansing of the Temple

MARK 11:11-26

*Friday of the Eighth Week of the Year*

Today's gospel has a lot of action in it, and a lot of confusion. The Temple, the fig tree, faith, forgiveness . . . all vie for our attention and prayer.

Let's think a bit about Jesus cleansing the Temple. He tells his onlookers that the Temple is meant to be a house of prayer for all people, but the seller and buyers have made it a den of thieves.

The temple of the church symbolized and represented so much for Jesus, as it does for us. It is the holy place, the place of peace where God is present and where we can find God.

Jesus will teach us that God dwells within all of us. By baptism we become the temple of the Holy Spirit, the dwelling place of God. As when we go to a church to be blessed and sanctified, so it is that when we go anywhere we bring blessing and the presence of God, for God dwells in us.

Our love is the little church where God dwells. God is present there because of the love that is found in the members of the family. Indeed, their love creates the Lord's presence. Where there is love, there is God's dwelling place. We know that when we enter some houses the warmth and the joy of God's love overwhelms us! Homes filled with photos of children and grandchildren tell us that there is so much love in this holy place. God is truly present.

If there's a lesson in all of this today, maybe it is that we have to be very careful to make sure that our house of God, our own minds and hearts, are kept pure and filled only with good things. We cannot allow anything to hurt us or make our hearts and minds the den of thieves.

We have to work hard at preserving our home as God's dwelling place and never allow anything or anyone to defile it or hurt it. Vigilant parents keep a check on what's on TV, what comes into their home, and the conversations that take place there. Our homes are all we have. They are the Lord's greatest blessing to us. It is in that little "church" that our children will learn all that they must about God's life and love.

## Jesus' Authority Is Questioned

MARK 11:27-33

*Saturday of the Eighth Week of the Year*

Jesus is beginning the final struggle with the religious authorities that will lead to his death. The clashes and tension between himself and the chief priests, scribes, and Pharisees will escalate until they reach the point of no return. It will be their survival or Jesus'! They will make sure that they survive. They will do anything. In all of this there is such a sadness in that the leaders can't see the good of the truth of Jesus; all they see is the threat to them and their position.

I think we all act in this way when someone treads on our turf. We aren't always appreciative of new ideas when they outshine ours. We get jealous of the new person who steals the attention and admiration of others, especially our superior.

The story of the establishment is the story of the establishment of most institutions and the absolute fear we have of anything new or novel. Unfortunately, over the centuries our own church has acted like the Jerusalem establishment, with dreadful results.

But aren't the chief priests and the leaders just like you and me? Aren't they good people who have given their lives to God and served God well? Haven't they lived the demands of the law in scrupulous observance? Weren't they sincere in believing Jesus was a blasphemer? Of course, to a point.

But there is also the point where we begin to worship the institution more than we do God. There is the point when we won't let the light in. We won't, or we can't, listen, see, or think. We become obsessed and idolatrous of an idea or institution. We are no longer human.

Let the sad lot of the priests, scribes, and Pharisees remind us all how human we are and how easy it is to give up thinking or judging for ourselves. Let us never miss embracing God's gift as they did, believing we are incapable of thinking, loving, and praying. Maybe the real sin against the Holy Spirit is to stop thinking for ourselves—what a sacrilege that is.

## The Parable of the Tenants

MARK 12:1-12

*Monday of the Ninth Week of the Year*

In this gospel story of the vineyard and the beloved son, Jesus tells a parable about God's love for the world by first sending prophets, who were rejected, and then finally sending God's only Son, who was also rejected and murdered. It's not a pleasant story, but it is our story and we should pay attention to it.

God has sent many people into our lives; saints and angels who have shared their love of God with us have touched us all. But, sometimes we won't, or we can't, listen to them. We consider the advice of a parent to be old-fashioned. We think of teachers and clergy as being "out of it." There are many wise and good people who touch our lives and who are truly the touch of our loving God, and we don't pay any attention to them. In reality, Jesus is present to us in so many experiences and people. When we reject Jesus in his servants, we reject Jesus himself and we dismiss him from our lives.

We have to be attentive to the presence and the call of Jesus in all of the events and people he sends to us each day. He is always speaking to us and waiting for our response. Many times we receive very positive and life-giving examples and encouragement. We must embrace them and use them to grow in this life. Sometimes we receive negative and even sinful stimuli. We must reject them and never allow them to corrupt the emotions and feelings of our heart. Nothing does more to dampen the spirit and bring sadness to our disposition and outlook than negativity. Never take negative people seriously. Avoid them like the plague. All they do is drag us down and make us as miserable as they are.

It is our duty each day to be the beacon of Christ's joy and peace to everyone we meet and everyone with whom we are in relationship. Even when we have to do something that challenges or corrects, do it with Christ's gentleness—never crush.

Never deliberately hurt another person. Never gossip or talk about anybody. Never! We are to be the prophets of his loving presence to others.

# Give to Caesar What Is Caesar's

MARK 12:13-17

*Tuesday of the Ninth Week of the Year*

The Pharisees and Herodians are out to trap Jesus in his speech. "Is it lawful to pay the tax, or not?" Two millennia later they are still up to their tricks as they trap us in our words and deeds. But the stage has changed.

As we scramble to give back to God what is God's, we often fail to give back to Caesar what is Caesar's. Catholics are still not exerting the influence on the social structure and public policy of this country that they should. For many of us, holiness consists in doing the things of the church. We are concerned with our prayer life, fulfilling our home responsibilities, and performing acts of charity to our neighbor. We have still not grasped that a major part of our morality is the doing of justice toward our neighbor and being workers for peace.

We still feel awkward in thinking of political elections and politics itself as being a part of the religious responsibility of a dedicated Christian. For us, morality still means sex. We have a long way to grow to understand that hungry children, war, poor education, capital punishment, and abortion are all very much issues of morality.

The Christian who is sincere in rendering to Caesar what is Caesar's is the person who is reading the newspapers, listening to politicians' speeches, writing letters to public officials, and, in general, involved in the life of our country.

For many of us it means going beyond a "church" morality and religion and embracing the struggle for justice and peace that every Christian must be a part of. We have so many wonderful examples to inspire us. People like Dorothy Day, Mother Teresa, Pope John Paul II, and Archbishop Romero remind us that we are our sisters' and brothers' keepers and that what we do to them we do to Christ.

Catholic social teaching inspires us to see Christ's work in all we do for our sisters and brothers who have no one to speak for them. Let us render to Caesar what is truly Caesar's!

## Marriage at the Resurrection

MARK 12:18-27

*Wednesday of the Ninth Week of the Year*

In today's gospel Jesus responds to the outlandish question of the Sadduccees about the poor widow who marries seven brothers in a row after each of them died. The brothers were being faithful to the command of Moses that directed a brother marry his brother's widow if he died childless in order to raise up progeny in his name.

We could well reflect on the gift of life and children and the resurrection to eternal life. While all of this is true enough, I wonder if the Jerusalem police ever investigated what this good woman was putting into her matzo ball soup that caused all of these gentlemen's demise!

In all fairness to this woman, I think she should have been canonized by the council of rabbis or at least have been given the Jerusalem equivalent of the Academy Award.

Maybe after all is said and done, what Jesus really wanted to do was to give us all a good laugh as we begin another day of grace.

# The Greatest Commandment

MARK 12:28-34

*Thursday of the Ninth Week of the Year*

"Which is the first of all the commandments?" Jesus is asked. He responds about loving God with all of our heart and soul and mind and strength. He then tells us that the second is very much like it: "Love your neighbor as yourself."

Perhaps the major reason that there is so little peace in the world today is that we are taking Jesus at his word and we are loving our neighbor as ourselves. That's the problem.

So many people don't love themselves as God loves them. So many don't believe in their own goodness, their possibilities, or that they deserve happiness in this world. So many torture themselves in guilt for their past lives. So many never achieve the peace and contentment that God wants them to have simply because they think they are not worthy.

This self-hatred is seen even in the guise of religion where people will see God as the lawgiver and judge and never as the forgiving and loving mother or father who cherishes, loves, and forgives us without limit or condition. So many have been given an image of God as hateful and evil, and they have never been able to overcome these early impressions and images. Some will make life decisions not based on what is good or best for them but on what they think they deserve given their past failures.

It is the church's role to call its people to embrace a loving God who will empower them to truly love themselves as God loves them. This change of heart will enable us to see ourselves as our God does, with love, tenderness, forgiveness, and hope. When we begin to cherish ourselves as our God does, then we can begin to do things that are good for our spiritual, emotional, and physical well-being. We will stop settling and begin to make choices worthy of who we are. We will begin to love ourselves.

As we grow in self-love we will become more self-giving, more compassionate, and more human. We will be able to love our neighbor with true and Christ-like love because we have first loved ourselves.

## The Son of David

MARK 12:35-37

*Friday of the Ninth Week of the Year*

Jesus touches today in the gospel on a very important aspect and title of his ministry. To be the Messiah is to be the Son of David, the descendant in the flesh of David, the great King and Shepherd of Israel. No one in the history of Israel is more revered and more loved by the people than David. In reality, when the Messiah comes, it will truly be David returning to them and David present to them in a new form. There is no salvation history without David. But what a complex figure David is. He's just like us.

As we reflect on his life, there should be so much to give us hope and encouragement. Just like us, David is capable of the most lofty and inspired relationship with God. He revels in God's goodness and love. As we pray his psalms at the Office and Mass each day, his words become the words of our deepest prayer and praise as they have been for our ancestors long before the coming of Christ.

The young and innocent shepherd boy kills the great Goliath with a slingshot. He is the model to us of the power of our goodness over the forces of evil. With God on our side we can conquer any evil. Nothing can overcome us—nothing but our own human frailty and weakness.

In David's case it was Bathsheba. He sees her and lusts after her. He commits adultery with her, fathers a child, and arranges to have Uriah killed in battle so that he can take her to himself and save his name, even at the cost of murdering his faithful friend and servant.

The innocent shepherd king becomes the adulterous, lying, and murdering king who denies and repudiates his holy anointing to choose what he desires rather than what God deserves. The broken, sinful king will eventually return in sorrow and peace to his God and be forgiven. His penitential psalms will describe his deep sorrow and God's forgiveness.

David is you and I. His story is our story. We have all had our great moments, our falls, our reconciliation, and our forgiveness. Just like David we have a God who loves us and will not allow our sins to separate us from him. Like the prodigal son and like David, the Lord gives us even greater blessings when we return to God and repent.

## The Widow's Offering

MARK 12:38-44

*Saturday of the Ninth Week of the Year*

Everyone's sweetheart is the poor widow. Jesus directs the apostles to what she is doing—she is giving God everything. She gives not from her excess, but from her very substance.

Money, in one form or another, is a very popular topic with Jesus. He mentions wealth many times in his talks and in his references to life and people's values. While I have always been touched by the generosity of the poor widow, I have grown to admire the other people who were putting large amounts into the treasury. I guess that as I've grown older and acquired a few dollars, I've learned a few things about money and myself.

When I've had little or nothing, giving away everything meant nothing. When I begin to accumulate something, all of a sudden I become possessive. Things like retirement and security all of a sudden become something I get concerned about. This becomes ludicrous when you realize that as a priest I'll always have a roof over my head and three square meals. My salary, while not great, is basically play money meant to be given away and shared with the poor. But the more I get, the more I want to hang on to it because I may need it for a rainy day. Having gone through the hurricanes and tornadoes of life and having come out of them just fine, why should I ever think the Lord would not take care of me on a rainy day?

When I see people in my parish who have dedicated a significant part of their income to the church and the poor (while paying college tuition and caring for parents), I can't help but be impressed and inspired to give back to God the first fruits of what God has given to me. Yes, I honestly feel that many of my beautiful people give much more than the poor widow.

Ten percent of a yearly salary of $100,000 is quite a commitment. The holy tithe guides many people's lives. I really hope that this is making you squirm a little. It is me. Maybe it's a good time to ask ourselves a basic question: "Does our increased prosperity help the poor as much as it should?" Are we as generous as we were when we had nothing?

*The*
*Gospel*
*According*
*to*
*Matthew*

# The Beatitudes

## MATTHEW 5:1-12

*Monday of the Tenth Week of the Year*

In today's gospel, Jesus sets out the agenda for his Kingdom and for our own personal fulfillment and happiness. He teaches us the beatitudes. If you visit the Mount of the Beatitudes on the Sea of Galilee, you breathe in the air and the atmosphere of this Kingdom. It is a beautiful place, lush and gently sloping down to the sea. It is a place that is a natural amphitheater, a place where you just want to recline on the lush grass and rest, a place where you would bring a picnic lunch and just enjoy the beauty of the Lord's creation and the goodness of people. It is a place that is in balance and at peace.

That is what the living of the beatitudes brings to us—balance and peace. The beatitudes are the criteria to judge and evaluate all that we are and all that we do as individuals and as church. The beatitudes are so simple and direct that they disarm us and can even terrorize us by their radical call to simplicity, justice, and love. That is what they are and that is what they demand. The beatitudes spell out the interpretations of the Golden Rule: "Do unto others as you would have others do unto you." They call us to live in peace and harmony with ourselves, our neighbor, and all of God's beautiful world.

And so Jesus calls us to simplicity and poverty of spirit. He calls us to make God's love our prized possession and for everything else to fit into its proper place after God. Jesus calls the sorrowing blessed for they imitate him in humble service. He calls those who hunger and thirst for justice—those who can never be at peace as long as their sisters and brothers are suffering—blessed. He calls the pure of heart blessed as they live with their eyes always fixed on God's Kingdom. He calls those who give their lives for people—the peacemakers—blessed. He calls those who suffer persecution for God's Kingdom blessed.

As we pray over the beatitudes, we have the plan of our life. We have our map. May the Lord give us the grace to follow it.

## Salt and Light

MATTHEW 5:13-16

*Tuesday of the Tenth Week of the Year*

In today's gospel, Jesus tells us that we are salt and light, the salt of the earth and light of the world, to be exact. Salt has certainly come upon bad times. No self-respecting health freak would be seen dead with a salt shaker in his or her hand. But be honest: Is there anything like salt on our freshly boiled Long Island corn or chilled, sliced home grown tomatoes? Of course not!

Salt is zest, passion, fun, and excitement. Did Jesus make a mistake in calling his church to be like salt? We seem to be anything but salty. Our worship, our teaching, our preaching, and our church itself is more often than not boring and tired.

Jesus is challenging us to let the power and the joy of the good news touch our hearts, our feelings, and our faces. Is there anything more contagious than the believer who is excited and happy about finding Jesus? What a difference it makes when a Christian is excited and wants to share the treasure with the world.

It's not that we don't believe, but how we believe— safely and gradually. We never want to tip our hand about how much Jesus means to us and how joyful we are to have been found by him and given another chance, over and over again.

May the salt and zest of our faith really influence us and give flavor to this world that is waiting for us to share this wonderful treasure of God's love.

The light of the world! We are the brightness of God's love shining forth and destroying all darkness, fear, and negativity. May we never be afraid of the dark, for Jesus, the Light, shines in our hearts. By faith and love we become the flame of love that cannot co-exist together with untruth, hatred, prejudice, or fear. We are the light that gives a point of hope and destiny to those who are lost and struggling. We are the light that brings the warmth and embrace of God's Love to the world.

The more we accept our call to be light and salt, the more the world changes and is transformed into the Kingdom of God. The Lord's salt and light bring hope and possibility to a world yearning to be excited by the good news of salvation.

## Teaching About the Law

MATTHEW 5:17-19

*Wednesday of the Tenth Week of the Year*

Jesus is the fulfillment of all of the promises of the past, and he is the hope of all the dreams of the future. He tells us in today's gospel that he has not come to destroy the law and the prophets but to fulfill them.

Jesus comes to us personally, not to destroy us, but to call us to the fullness of our own promise. In the spiritual life, there is great stress on the rooting out of vices and the destruction of sin. Maybe we emphasize the wrong thing in our journey to Christ. Instead of emphasizing the negative aspect of our vices, perhaps we should look more to redirect them and re-channel them to Christ.

In each of the traditional capital sins we find a life-giving energy. How we direct it and use it is the difference between virtue and sin. The same energy that drives us to lust has in it the possibility of our being loving, chaste, warm, and compassionate. We cannot destroy the energy. It is how God made us. It is our very life force; there is no life without it. Without it we are emotionally dead.

Herein lies the dilemma. All too often the alternative to vice and sin becomes a sterile, dead, lackluster, sexless, moral conformity. Virtue without passion is not virtue. It is simply non-involved, emotionless existence. It is not life.

Mother Teresa is a beautiful example of creative energy leading to tremendous and passionate involvement, kindness, and the most loving person one could ever become. Mother Teresa could have used all those energies for evil and selfishness, but she chose to allow the Spirit to call her to creative chastity.

As we journey to the Lord, we deal with our demons: pride, covetousness, envy, greed, lust, sloth, anger. We have the ability to direct the energy of each of these to virtue and life. We saw the lust-to-love conversion of a Mother Teresa. Pride can flower into a real sense of self-worth; covetousness and greed into true appreciation of the beauty and value of things. Envy can turn into a healthy admiration and imitation of good; sloth into savoring the beauty of the moment. Jesus has not come to destroy but to fulfill. He does not want us to destroy ourselves. He wants us to bring ourselves to completion and perfection by turning the energy of how we are created to goodness and life.

## Teaching About Anger

MATTHEW 5:20-26

*Thursday of the Tenth Week of the Year*

Jesus calls us closer to God's love today as he brings us beyond the commandments. He expects more from us than not killing or not hurting our neighbor. He demands that we all do what we can to live in peace with ourselves and our neighbor. Jesus is setting forth his peace plan that demands a total change of heart.

Jesus tells us that if we are bringing our gift to the altar and realize as we are doing so that we have something against our brother or sister, we should first go and make peace with him or her and then offer the gift at the altar. This is such basic common sense teaching. Yet how often we miss the point and complicate the meaning of Jesus' teaching.

In so many churches, the eucharist is offered day in and day out, Sunday after Sunday. We come, we hear the sermon, and we say all of the prayers. Then we go home and pick up where we left off. We continue to harbor feelings of resentment and hatred. We are content to remain angry at friends and family members. Somewhere along the line, we just never got it. We never got the part that eucharist demands forgiveness, healing and letting go of the past.

The eucharist is meant to be the prime sacrament of forgiveness and healing. Each time we prepare our hearts to hear the word of God, it is demanded that we also be open to conversion and new beginnings.

The most obvious requirement for receiving the eucharist is that, to the best of our ability, we are at peace with all people. It demands that we let go of the shackles that are holding us back from forgiveness. It demands that we be in the process of forgiving anyone who has hurt us in any way at all.

The eucharist, if intelligently received, demands a change of heart and a completely new way of thinking and acting toward our neighbor. It means putting down our gifts, going back to be reconciled, and then returning to offer our gift. All this means that we recognize the Lord Jesus in the breaking of the bread.

# Teaching About Adultery and Divorce

## MATTHEW 5:27-32

*Friday of the Tenth Week of the Year*

In today's gospel, Jesus calls us to purity of actions and purity of mind and heart. This call and message of Jesus to avoid not only the action of adultery but even deliberate and private adulterous thoughts is, to say the least, countercultural.

It is a tall order for us in a world where everything from toothpaste to cars is sold through advertising that portrays the semi-nude bodies of women or even the sexual embrace of a couple. Sex is everywhere—TV, books, magazines. In almost every TV program we see, it is presumed that the meeting of any man or woman is going to end up with them going to bed. As this casual sexual activity is presumed for everyone, even our teenagers, Jesus seems to be calling us into a morality and standard that is totally beyond us.

As we try to keep our actions, thoughts, and desires in the Lord's direction, we are actually placing our whole lives in the Kingdom of God, and we are placing the totality of who and what we are, including sex, in God's hands.

One cannot live the Christian life without the grace of God. We cannot love, forgive, reconcile, and be chaste only by our own power. To walk with the Lord demands that our hearts and lives be constantly open to his touch.

God has given us the gift of sexuality. We place it in God's hands and ask for the grace each day to live it out according to our vocation. Whether we are married, single, widowed, divorced, celibate, gay, or straight, we cannot be chaste without the grace of God. Temptation is part of the beauty of humanity. Struggle is part of our loving.

Impure thoughts are unavoidable. What we do with temptation is the measure of our love. They will always come into our minds. Remember, we can't prevent the birds from flying over our heads, but that doesn't mean we allow them to nest in our hair! Temptation, struggle, and even falling is one thing—surrender is another!

## Teaching About Oaths

MATTHEW 5:33-37

*Saturday of the Tenth Week of the Year*

Today's gospel about taking oaths is another instruction of Jesus about being people of the light and of the truth. It is the call of Jesus to be people who walk in the light and who can be completely open and transparent in all that we are and all that we do.

Jesus is telling us that for the person of true integrity, there should never be a need of taking an oath to guarantee telling the truth. We are to be people of complete truthfulness who would never even think of lying or being false.

Jesus tells us to say "yes" when we mean "yes" and "no" when we mean "no." "Say what you mean and mean what you say."

It is so rare to see people actually living and relating in such openness and truthfulness. Even in church settings one can find game playing, deviousness, and untruthfulness.

To be really honest, there has to be an atmosphere of trust and acceptance. No one is going to open their hearts and become vulnerable where they feel they will be attacked because of their candor. What Jesus calls us to is more than just the truth. He calls us to the kind of relationships and community where we feel affirmed for telling the truth.

The prophet will speak the truth no matter where or to whom. The prophet cannot but speak the truth regardless of the outcome.

Let us ask the Lord for the gift to speak his truth no matter what. Let us ask for the gift to speak it in charity and sensitivity. Let us also pray for a church and a world that is a real community where to speak the truth is the easiest and most natural thing to do.

## An Eye for an Eye

MATTHEW 5:38-42

*Monday of the Eleventh Week of the Year*

Today's gospel would bring an ear-to-ear grin on the face of the likes of Dorothy Day. It proclaims total and absolute non-violence and pacifism. It is one of the gospels that is read at Mass and quickly put to the side or always explained by saying that Jesus really didn't mean it literally, which of course, he did.

Offer no resistance, offer the other cheek to be struck, hand over your coat, walk for the two miles instead of one! With these short little phrases Jesus is enduring all the principles that hold together state and church. The life and ethic Jesus is calling us to is far more radical and revolutionary than anything we have actually lived at any time in our history as a church.

The best we ever seem to be able to put forward is one, maybe two, Catholics who are radical Christians who live the gospel just as it is with no tampering or watering it down. We have our St. Francises, Dorothy Days, and Mother Teresas throughout our history. The rest of us, from popes to parents, all settle for a far easier and much more practical brand of Christianity that doesn't really push us much beyond our comfort zone.

We have as a church reinvented Jesus and Christianity to suit our own needs and maybe our own abilities to live the radical call to the gospel. We don't follow the Jesus of the gospel and his call to poverty and pacifism. We invent "just war" theories and we gently correct Jesus on his impracticality about money and what it can buy.

It would at least be a healthy thing if personally and institutionally we could confess our inability to live the gospel as presented. That would be confessing that we are all living in a state of sin, but maybe that is the best we can do for now and we have to rely on the merciful love of our Savior who accepts and still loves us in our sinfulness. He is satisfied with us and never casts us away, even though we don't even begin to live up to the gospel demands.

## Loving Our Enemies

MATTHEW 5:43-48

*Tuesday of the Eleventh Week of the Year*

In today's gospel Jesus tells us that we must become perfect, as our heavenly Father is perfect. How do we reach that perfection? We do so by loving our enemies and by praying for those who persecute us. Jesus asks for the impossible, or at least it seems that way for most of us.

As the teaching of Jesus draws on and deepens in the Sermon of the Mount, Jesus is taking us into waters we have never been in before. His hearers of two thousand years ago, along with his hearers of today, are faced with a quandary in which we know that we can't do what Jesus asks of us by our own power or grace. It literally requires a miracle of grace to be able to make such a leap in faith that we want to begin the process of loving and reconciliation.

In this gospel, Jesus is talking about the victim forgiving the abuser. He is talking about a family forgiving the murderers of their child. He is talking about a Jewish survivor of the Holocaust forgiving the Germans. He is talking about the Jews and Arabs, the Moslems and

Christians in Yugoslavia, and the Catholics and Protestants in Northern Ireland.

Jesus is asking us to follow him from the somewhat safe risks of forgiveness and love within the tribe and family to a new and universal outlook of love and forgiveness for all people.

How could we ever love or forgive the way Jesus demands us to? Well, we don't start with dramatic forgiveness. We start with our daily and simple walk with Jesus in discipleship. We walk with Jesus each day. The word of God nourishes us as it begins to soften our hearts in little things. It is in this way that we grow and become capable of greater things.

Jesus gives the power and grace of his Holy Spirit to those who seek out his will and his direction each day. It is not a dramatic event; it is a gradual and gentle growth into a new and abundant life.

We grow beyond polite forgiveness and love as we allow his heart to gradually rule ours. When we are challenged by our inability to love or forgive, the place to begin the process is at his feet in prayer. He will help us to do the impossible.

The process may take all of our life, but if we are faithful to the walk with Jesus we will find that we have become new creations by his love and that nothing is impossible to us because our heart has become the heart of Jesus.

## Do Not Act Like the Hypocrites

MATTHEW 6:1-6, 16-18

*Wednesday of the Eleventh Week of the Year*

Today's gospel is the gospel we read on Ash Wednesday at the beginning of Lent. On Ash Wednesday so many people come to church ready to do many and beautiful things for Jesus. They want to show their love for Jesus by acts of prayer, charity, and mortification. On that great day of the ashes, Jesus warns us about pride and vanity in doing these things and reminds us that we have to do them for him and not for people's applause.

It's not always easier to do things just for Jesus. It feels good to know that someone we respect and love thinks we're good and that we're doing something worthwhile. It helps to know that most holy people struggle with this. There's a part of them that wants to do that act of kindness totally anonymously, but it's nice to know that someone respects what we're doing. It's beautiful to pray the scriptures, but sometimes it really helps if somebody else sees us with the New Testament or Office Book in our hands as we ride the train to work.

We used to talk about "purity of intention." That meant that we did nothing except praise and honor God. We tried to remove every human and selfish motivation from what we did so that our only motivation was the glory of God.

Know what? It can't be done! No action by anyone is totally pure. All that we do is a contradiction to many motivations and desires. There is no such thing as perfect purity or motivation this side of heaven.

So what can we do? Our best. We give the Lord who and what we are and what we do. We give God our beauty, impurity and purity, noble and ignoble reasons and motivations, and we let God forgive it all out of us and do with it what God wants. In our brokenness and weakness all we can offer the Lord is our love (as mixed up and complicated and impure as that is!) and know that God understands and will do the best thing possible with it for us and for the church.

We have a Redeemer who loves us, forgives us, and is delighted with what we place in his hands, as flawed as we might think it is.

# The Lord's Prayer

MATTHEW 6:7-15

*Thursday of the Eleventh Week of the Year*

Jesus teaches us the Lord's Prayer. We pray this holy and beautiful prayer before communion. Jesus has given us a model of what all prayer should be rather than teaching us a formula of a particular prayer.

The Lord's Prayer is meant to flow from our hearts. It is not the rattling off of eloquent or special words that will impress God. Words will never impress God, only the sincerity and the love of our hearts. It has to be the expression of all that we believe in, all that we love, and all that we hope for. Our prayer doesn't even need words. Sometimes they get in the way of a pure heart just being enthralled to be in the presence of the Lord. The beat of a loving heart is the most eloquent prayer that can be offered to God.

Jesus is not teaching the form of prayer; he is teaching its substance. Prayer flows from relationship. God is our Father. The love that the Father has for Jesus he has for us. "As the Father has loved me, so do I love you." Our Father doesn't love us as he might love some inferior but pleasant being like the way we love our pets. The Father loves us in a passionate and total way. So great is this love that the Father gave his only Son to enter our human condition and to become part of it forever in Jesus.

The Father is like the widow looking for the coin, like the shepherd seeking the lost sheep, and like the father waiting for the return of the prodigal son. Our Father is delighted when we come to him. He rejoices when we begin to pray: "Our Father." We bring joy and pleasure to the God of Love when we open our hearts to him in prayer.

Let us not hide behind words. Let nothing stand in the way of embracing this passionate God of Love who loves us and believes in us and forgives us beyond our wildest yearnings. Our journey to conversion is to come closer to believing that he loves us so. When we do, then we will be able to pray the Lord's Prayer.

## Treasures in Heaven
MATTHEW 6:19-23

*Friday of the Eleventh Week of the Year*

What are the most important things in your life? If you had to leave your home and could bring along only one thing, what would it be? Whom do you love so much that you would lay down your life for him or her here and now? The answer to these questions is the answer to "Where is your treasure?"

Our very complicated lives need a center, a focus if you will, that will give proper perspective and direction to all that we do and all that we seek. Our center is Christ. Our relationship with him in faith and love is what gives meaning to all that we do.

Our job, our family, our education, our projects, our dreams—everything has to flow from this relationship. If we work at making and keeping Christ at the center of our lives, then amazing things happen in our lives.

Relationally, we change. We have to be a better husband, wife, parent, friend, sister, brother, or priest when Christ gives meaning to what we are. When we try to make him our first love, we are able to love more deeply and more generously than before. We are able to relate and interact with everyone in a healthier and more human way because we have become healthier and more human knowing Jesus Christ.

Materially, we look at things differently. We come to appreciate that everything is a gift of God and that all

God's gifts are meant to praise and serve God. If the Lord has blessed us with financial success, we know that we have a responsibility to share these gifts with the poor. We do not make money and things as an end in themselves, but we use them to praise and serve the Lord.

We must never allow things to possess us. We must possess them and see a special responsibility to justice and charity according to our blessings.

Our real treasure must always be love, mercy, compassion, generosity, and kindness. Rust and moths cannot consume them. They can only grow more brilliant and beautiful. They are the true stepping stones into the heavenly Kingdom. No one can ever take them away from us, for they belong to the Lord.

O Lord, let our hearts always be with you and with the treasure that will never be lost—your love.

## "All These Things Will Be Given You"

### MATTHEW 6:24-34

*Saturday of the Eleventh Week of the Year*

A story about the gospel:

Bennie would love to own Mr. DiCarlo's Pizzeria. He has worked for him for three years and has really gotten the hang of making pizzas. The customers love them, and no one is ever satisfied with the single slice they promise to limit themselves to for lunch. Pretty girls (who love to flirt with Bennie, who doesn't mind a bit) watching their weight and overweight businessmen all seem to turn lunchtime into a feast.

Bennie did more than make and sell pizza. He really connected with people. Lunchtime at DiCarlo's Pizzeria turned into a family meal where everyone got to know and like one another through the catalyst named Bennie. Everyone got to know a lot about everyone else: who was having a baby, who was leaving for college, who was in the hospital, who died—all this was common knowledge to the pizzeria lunch crowd. Frequently a hat was passed around to help somebody who was in a jam. While Bennie didn't own the pizzeria, he became the *de facto* proprietor.

Bennie took the time to draw out the hurting, the shy, and the lonely. He looked into their eyes and smiled and said, "Can I help you?" People saw that he meant it. Even if he couldn't really do anything for them, just being in the pizzeria kidding and bantering with him made them feel better.

One of DiCarlo's frequenters was Lou. Lou was a down and out old bum who reeked to high heaven. Even the garlic, cheese, and tomato sauce couldn't conceal the pungency of Lou when he walked in. Of course, he never had any money, and, of course, Bennie would always give him a few slices and a can of soda. Bennie did it in such a way that nobody, including Mr. DiCarlo, knew that he had no money. Bennie always justified it to himself by reasoning that it was just a few slices that didn't have to be thrown out at night. The fact that Lou reminded Bennie of his dad didn't hurt either. And anyway, what the hell, the old guy gulped down his lunch.

One particularly cold night, Bennie was working the late shift getting ready to close up at 11:00. There was a whole pizza left over when who should appear at five minutes to eleven but our Lou. "Hey, how ya doin', Champ?" Bennie greeted Lou. "Not bad, Benedict." (Lou loved to be formal. Bennie was sure he must have gone to college.) Bennie looked down at the whole pizza—all eight slices with sausage and meatballs on top of melted cheese. "Lou, can you use a whole pizza?" "You betcha! Benedict, I have some friends who'd love some."

Lou put the steaming pizza in a box and threw in an open bottle of Chianti and some cups. As Bennie handed Lou the pizza and the wine he saw tears in Lou's eyes. "Good night, Benedict. God bless you!"

Bennie quickly closed up and locked the front door of the pizzeria. It must have been 20°, and it began to snow. Bennie walked around the back to the parking lot to get his car. He looked across the lot to the garbage dumpster and saw a sight he'd never forget. Seated on a box and surrounded by all the cats and dogs of the neighborhood was Lou feasting on pizza with sausage and meatballs. Like a bolt of lightning, Bennie realized that Lou had no home to bring pizza to. The spot next to the dumpster was his residence.

Bennie walked over to Lou, whose face beamed into a broad smile when he saw him. "Bennie, will you join us?" " I sure will," Bennie said. Bennie sat down near Lou on a box generously vacated by a cat who didn't seem to mind. "Will you have a slice, Benedict?" "You bet I will," responded Bennie.

Lou broke off a piece of his slice of pizza and gave it to Bennie with a cup of wine. This time there were tears in Bennie's eyes.

" . . . and they recognized the Lord Jesus in the breaking of the bread."

## Judging Others

MATTHEW 7:1-5

*Monday of the Twelfth Week of the Year*

Today Jesus warns us about being too quick in judging others. Indeed he tells us that if we want to avoid being judged ourselves, we must avoid judging others.

This admonition of Jesus is a difficult one. After all, we are always making judgments about what people are saying and what they are doing. There is an obligation to distance ourselves from people, places, and things that are not good for us. We used to call them the occasion of sin: people, places, and things that would or could lead us away from the Lord's way to another that would hurt us.

We are always making judgments about the places we frequent. We *know* because we *judge* that some situations are too much for us to handle. We judge about the appropriateness of certain cable networks coming into our homes. We avoid certain people who drag us down. It seems that the Christian has to judge a lot of things and make decisions according to the light of the . . .

But Jesus is not speaking about that kind of mature Christian judging here. Jesus is speaking of the hypocritical looking down on people as if they were below us and using judgment as a way of pretending that we are superior to another.

This type of judging delights in the weaknesses and failures of another. It is the sick and perverse exposing and harping upon the failures of a sister or brother. This activity makes us feel superior and it absolves us of the need to look at our own sinfulness.

We can take the example of someone who is in an adulterous relationship. Our good judgment will make us more aware that what this person is doing is wrong and can ruin his or her life. We hate the sin. We don't go around spreading gossip about the person. *We pray for the sinner*. If we can offer loving counsel to them and try to help them out of the situation, we do so. *We love the sinner*.

We know that but for the grace of God there go we. We know that we are no better than this person, maybe luckier, maybe much more blessed and thus more accountable for our own actions.

Jesus commands us to do a thorough job on ourselves before we attempt to help another person. People who are not concerned about removing the plank from their own eyes have very little time to try removing the speck from a neighbor's eye.

# Pearls Before Swine

## MATTHEW 7:6, 12-14

*Tuesday of the Twelfth Week of the Year*

In today's gospel, Jesus continues to teach us, sharing the beautiful wisdom of the Sermon on the Mount. He begins by warning us about giving holy things to dogs and casting our pearls before swine. We learn here that the word of God is sacred and should be proclaimed only in the situations where it at least will not be mocked. In a sense, we have to know our audience. There is a natural progression to preaching and teaching the word.

In the work scene, evangelization doesn't begin by walking into an office with an open bible asking people to accept Jesus. It begins with the disciple of Jesus walking into a situation and being a Christian. We evangelize by working honestly and well at our job. We touch people by being a good co-worker and friend as time passes. When we live in such a way that Jesus is at the center of all we do, we have prepared the field to sow the seed of his love in the hearts of others.

Evangelization is a process. It takes a long time. It flows from relationship and witness, not the other way around. This is also true in parish life. The priest, sister, deacon, and lay minister preach the word not just in their sermons, classes, or ministry; they preach it primarily by their love of their people and their desire to be part of that community.

All of the wonderful and up-to-date programs and ministries are doomed to fail if they lack the one absolutely essential ingredient: love. There is no substitute for the minister loving his or her people. They give the community permission to love one another by loving the community first.

The celebration of the eucharist is only ritual and externals unless the people who celebrate it are truly a family. The deeper the bond of love and service in the community, the more powerful is the presence of Jesus to his people.

It is a wonderful thing in today's church to see more and more people professionally trained for ministry. When that expertise is wedded to a deep and loving commitment to the people we serve, it is a holy and beautiful thing.

Sometimes, we who minister can become the dogs and swine when we forget who it is we minister to: Jesus. Let us treat our people with the same love, gestures, respect, and compassion we could have for Jesus.

## False Prophets

MATTHEW 7:15-20

*Wednesday of the Twelfth Week of the Year*

The Lord warns us today about the danger of false prophets and being deceived by what appears to be wonderful and attractive but is in reality dangerous and destructive.

If there were ever a time when evil was made to seem attractive and wonderful, it is now. The communications explosion from the printed page to television, music, film, and the Internet is packed daily with seductive and untruthful images that need to be discerned and judged in the light of Jesus. It is becoming more and more difficult to choose what is right and to make judgments that are consistent with what we know and believe.

Certainly our prayer life is a very important part of this process, but just as important is the need to open our hearts to Christian and loving friends, to spiritual direction and the sacrament of reconciliation, and to counseling. Twelve-step programs are often a great help in this area. So many people's lives have been changed because they were able to confess to a group: "I am an alcoholic."

We need other people. We need people we can trust and rely upon to guide us through making right decisions. When people are truly honest and will open their hearts to another, beautiful and life-giving things happen.

Jesus doesn't want us to walk the journey all by ourselves. The greater the person, the more disposed they are to open their hearts to another in the journey to God's will. Most holy people never make decisions of great importance without first discussing them with a person they know is open to God's Spirit and walks with Jesus.

So many things are just not black or white. Most are gray and most require a prayerful and humble discernment to truly find the loving pleasure of God. When we make our decision in this prayerful and dialogic manner we *know* that we have to be making the right decision. The actual decision is not what really matters; it is the process in coming to that decision that matters. The process is always walking through it with Jesus and the community. It is there that the Holy Spirit will guide us, and it is there that we can recognize the wolf in sheep's clothing.

## The True Disciple

MATTHEW 7:21-29

*Thursday of the Twelfth Week of the Year*

The message of Jesus in today's gospel is most direct: you do not enter the Kingdom of God by what you say but by who and what you are. Actions speak louder than words. While this message is important to all Christians, it really is imperative for all who are in Christian ministry. From being parents, lay ministers, priests, etc., there is a very important message to all of us.

It is very important to be a good minister, but it is *more* important to be a good Christian. As we grow as a faith community, the church is putting more and more effort into professionally training all its ministers, priestly and otherwise. That is a wonderful thing for the church!

What a blessing it is to see more and more people trained in preaching and teaching the word. What a blessing it is to see more and more people trained in theology, liturgy, scripture, and administration. But how dangerous it is if our future priests and future ministers are not first formed in the principles of the spiritual life, which is really the gospel life of Jesus.

It does the church incredible harm if the people who preach and teach and lead are not the embodiment of what it means to be another Christ. Before we teach a class or minister to a person we must be women and men of truth, justice, compassion, forgiveness, and integrity. When church people become petty, small-minded, gossipy, uncharitable, disrespectful, and condescending to their peers and to their people, much of the power of their message is lost and neutralized. Fr. Mike McLoughlin, the spiritual director of the Immaculate Conception Seminary in Huntington, gave my classmates and me a message I have never forgotten. He told us that what we are shouts so loud that no one can hear what we say or preach.

He was right. Before we make grandiose plans for our parishes, perhaps we have to first make sure that we are faithful to the daily, humble following of Jesus and that the most important thing in our lives is imitating and following Jesus in all that we do.

# Jesus Cleanses a Leper

### MATTHEW 8:1-4

*Friday of the Twelfth Week of the Year*

Today, Jesus meets the leper. His prayer is so humble and simple: "Sir, if you will to do so, you can cure me." Jesus responded, "I will do it. Be cured."

When was the last time that you asked Jesus right out to cure you? I find that I pussyfoot around Jesus with my needs, pray about all sorts of things, but seldom just honestly and truthfully tell Jesus what my problem is and ask him to cure it. Why is that? Am I afraid of his saying "No"? Am I so lacking in faith that he really can do it or that maybe he doesn't love me enough to heal me? I don't know.

Maybe there's another part of this that I don't want to face. If I ask Jesus to cure me, it is not asking that friendly magician from Nazareth to wave the magic wand and make it all better. Healing has a much deeper and more significant meaning.

If I sincerely ask Jesus to cure me I am in effect giving my life to him and also committing myself to do what is necessary for the healing to be complete. When I give my life to Jesus, I am saying that I will take the healing as Jesus sees best for me. That might mean that being healed from cancer might bring me graces in my life with God, rather than the end of the physical cancer. What I am saying (if I am his real disciple) is that I want to be healed, but if it is better for me and the church that I *not* be healed, I accept that too! You can see that it takes a real relationship of faith to be able to mean that!

If we ask Jesus to heal us of alcohol, drug, sex, or another addiction, it means that we will use all the means that he places at our disposal. We have to work on a twelve-step program. We have to use counseling, spiritual direction, and confession. We must do our part to bring about the healing. We must ask, but we must do. Again, action means more than words. By all means we should come to Jesus.

## The Faith of the Centurion

MATTHEW 8:5-17

*Saturday of the Twelfth Week of the Year*

The words of the centurion in today's gospel have been immortalized by our church. We pray them at each Mass before we receive holy communion: "Lord, I am not worthy to receive you but only say the word and I shall be healed." Jesus is amazed at the faith of the centurion, but it seems that Jesus was always much more successful in touching the hearts of those who were "on the outs." In the mystery of grace, the non-believer often believes much more deeply than those who "practice" the faith, and the fruits of the Holy Spirit seem much more evident in their lives. The centurion speaks for each one of us—single parent, divorced, happily married, unhappily married, homosexual—all of us. "I am not worthy"—please just say the word and I shall be healed. The most beautiful moment of the week occurs when all the unworthy gather around the table and come to be fed. This meal is no reward for good or moral living, it is rather the sharing of the life and love of the One who loves us without condition and is delighted to say but the word. We *are* healed! We *are* forgiven!

In this past week we've prayed a lot about struggles, uncertainty, failure, and growth. In all the struggles, Jesus has been there.

There is no more holy moment than when we come home to Jesus in holy communion. We come with the prayer of the centurion: "Lord, I am not worthy," and with the prayer of the leper, "Sir, if you will to do so, you can cure me."

Let us open our hearts to the One who loves us so much, does not judge or condemn us, but constantly invites us to love and accept him as our brother and Savior.

## The Cost of Following Jesus

MATTHEW 8:18-22

*Monday of the Thirteenth Week of the Year*

Today's gospel finds Jesus spelling out very clearly what it will cost to be his disciple. It is not easy. It demands a lot—our whole life and everything that we possess.

In this gospel reading, Jesus tells the would-be disciple that following him will mean possessing nothing, not even a place to sleep, and that he and the gospel come before human relationships, even the burying of one's parents.

It is one of the gospel imperatives that we all dance around as we try explain away the fact that we don't follow them. The simple truth is that at any time in the church's life there are only a handful of Christians who follow to the letter what Jesus taught. Even those who do follow the gospel commands will confess that they are not following them; Dorothy Day and Mother Teresa would be the first to confess that they didn't live up to the full gospel demands.

So what should the rest of us do? Squirm! Squirm and listen again to yesterday's gospel in which Jesus told us not to judge. Maybe the next time that we are tempted to judge and condemn the poor teenager who has an abortion we can think about ourselves living our luxurious lifestyles, "eye of the needle" words of Jesus not withstanding.

So we squirm and water down and rationalize the Lord's demands for discipleship by talking about the "spirit" of poverty. It makes us feel better to do that because the truth is we're not capable of following all his demands.

Let us at least, then, *not* be too ready to condemn another when we all have our own baggage of sin and imperfection that we live with. Our tendency is to create our own "OK" sins in our own lifestyle. We do that by saying that we know what Jesus *said*, but we know what he really *meant*.

In the full picture of God's loving understanding and mercy, I think God is much less pleased by a rich priest or materialistic church than by the prostitute selling his or her body to live. I hope this makes you as uncomfortable as it does me. That's what the gospel is supposed to do. At least let us use generously and lovingly the things that a poor servant of Jesus shouldn't have. Let us make the poor our best friends. In so doing the Lord will overlook a lot of our failures and let us realize by pondering on today's gospel that discipleship has real price attached to it: our lives.

## Calming the Storm

### MATTHEW 8:23-27

*Tuesday of the Thirteenth Week of the Year*

Would we like to have Jesus in our boat during a storm at sea? Of course we would. There are so many moments in our lives when we feel better and safer when the people we love are by our side. Isn't this the tremendous power of family and friends? Just by their being there, things are better and we feel more secure and less afraid. We have grown up knowing this from being infants in our parents' arms to having friends stand by us in the death of those same parents—presence, touch, and love change the terrible into the beautiful.

113

The disciples on the boat with Jesus didn't quite understand that the very presence of Jesus, even taking forty winks, was their safety. Jesus asks them where their courage is and tells them they have so little faith.

I think we're like the disciples. We *know* he's by our side in the storms, yet we need reassurance. We need him to touch us, to speak to us, and to reassure us. We need to feel his presence and to hear his voice.

When we allow Jesus to be present to us in our daily non-turbulent life, we have much more chance of hearing and experiencing him in the turbulent days and seasons. A daily nourishment of the word of God and daily prayer of the heart to Jesus disposes us to be always open and present to his touch and love.

We have a true and living relationship with the Lord. He belongs to us and we to him. But every relationship has to be cultivated. We have to reach out on a daily basis so that we can feel and experience the love that is always there for us. When we live in this way we are always aware of and present to the touch and love of Jesus in our lives.

At the word of Jesus the storm is quieted. No matter what is going on outside of us our heart is calm and we are at peace because Jesus has touched us and he is with us. Jesus brings us through the storm. He keeps us safe, and he delivers us.

We are invited to rest in the tranquility of his love. Our daily prayers change everything in our lives. We know what truly matters, and we are never afraid because his love casts out all fear. Daily we love him as daily he touches us.

# Jesus Heals the Gadarene Demoniacs

MATTHEW 8:28-34

*Wednesday of the Thirteenth Week of the Year*

Have you ever had a day when you said to Jesus what the swineherders said to him in today's gospel: "Leave us alone!" "Go away!" They couldn't comprehend what this was all about. All they knew was that their swine were dead and their livelihood was dashed. The fact the swine were driven by the demons cast out of the two men didn't interest the townspeople at all. All they knew was that this Jesus caused them trouble and they were better off without him, or so they thought.

Jesus certainly didn't win any points with the demons who were forced to set the townsmen free. They wound up where they belonged—in the swine drowning in the sea.

The only "winners" in this gospel are the two men who were touched by the mercy of Jesus and set free. Jesus heard their cry, saw their misery, and called two sons of God to freedom and to begin a new life.

With all of the conflicting elements of this gospel, this seems to be the thing that matters. Jesus reaches out to the poorest of the poor, and he invites us to imitate his example in our dealings with one another.

In the long run, love will conquer hate, and good will overcome evil. Jesus has won the war, but the battles are still being fought in the areas of our hearts. As hard as the fray may become, we know that with Jesus we are victors and he will never allow the Evil One to overcome us. His love conquers all things.

# Jesus Heals a Paralytic

MATTHEW 9:1-8

*Thursday of the Thirteenth Week of the Year*

This story of the paralytic is so touching at so many levels. If this poor man didn't have friends, he would never have met Jesus. Isn't it wonderful to have friends who will carry us to meet Jesus? It is such a consoling prayer to praise and thank the Lord for all those people in our lives who have carried us to Jesus. In each of our lives there are those people who have loved us so much that they carried us when we just couldn't make it on our own. There are people who have loved us so much that we know we would not and could not be who we are if they hadn't been there for us.

When people love us so much that they carry us to Jesus, we have already met him in their love. Their love is a sacrament of Christ's love, and we have already been touched by him in their holy touch. We become the sacrament of healing as we attempt to bring one another to Jesus. His ministry grows as his disciples share his love and compassion with others.

The story tells us that when Jesus saw their faith he said, "Have courage, son, your sins are forgiven." The faith of the paralytic's friends brings about the miracle of forgiveness and healing that this man receives. How powerful faith is. It is almost irresistible to Jesus. He acts because these people believe in him, not because the paralytic does.

Jesus gives him the gift he really needs—he forgives the paralytic's sins. It was not the physical ailment that was paralyzing this man, it was the spiritual. Jesus lifted the burden of sin and guilt from his heart and made him a free man. What a gift he received that day!

Then, to complete the cure and silence the scribes, he told the man to stand up, roll up his mat, and go home.

Jesus gave the man his healing, but it was quickly followed by a job. Go home! Get on with your life. Love, live, and help build the Kingdom, and in so doing you will carry others who are paralyzed in body, mind, and spirit.

## The Call of Matthew

MATTHEW 9:9-13

*Friday of the Thirteenth Week of the Year*

In today's gospel Jesus calls Matthew. The summons is so clear and definite, "Follow me." Matthew, the tax collector's response is just as definite. Matthew got up from his past and followed Jesus. The rest is history.

That night Matthew had a dinner party in honor of Jesus. The disciples were there and so were all of Matthew's old friends and drinking buddies. They were there to celebrate this Jesus who called Matthew to follow him. What a party it must have been! What a group of characters! Imagine the language and the tall stories. And there is Jesus in the middle of it all, loving it and making everyone feel right at home.

When Jesus is criticized for eating with sinners, he tells the Pharisees the purpose of his ministry: he has come to call sinners, not the self-righteous.

The scene of the supper is the model for what will be known as the eucharist. The eucharist is the meal that Jesus gives for all of us, but most of all for sinners. It is the meal where everyone is welcome and everyone has a spot, right next to Jesus. It is the meal that includes everyone and brings hope to all.

We all know that no one is worthy to sit at the table. We all know that we are not worthy to receive holy communion. No one ever was or ever will be. We are there because the Divine Lover has invited us and we belong there. We are his family, his sisters and brothers. He could never cast us aside.

Our prayer is that of the centurion: "Lord, I am not worthy for you to enter into my house. Just say the word and I will be healed." The eucharist continues to call all people together at the Lord's table. As we share in his life and love, we leave the table to bring the Jesus we have received into our lives and work. We who have received the eucharist *become* the eucharist for the world.

## The Question About Fasting

MATTHEW 9:14-17

*Saturday of the Thirteenth Week of the Year*

Today's gospel speaks of two topics that are at the heart of Christianity—feasting and fasting. They are a big part of our own lives, or at least they should be. Jesus is criticized because he was always feasting. His main vehicle of evangelization was table ministry. He was constantly accepting invitations to dinner from everybody, the rich and poor and the saints and sinners. He sat down at anyone's table so that they could experience firsthand the presence of God's love and call in their lives.

Fasting was also part of the life of Jesus. The desert experience was very important for his preparation for ministry. There were many times that he had to be alone to pray and fast. Unfortunately, in our own lives, we've lost the ability to really feast or to truly fast. Somewhere in the middle we find ourselves doing neither, but operating on automatic pilot in which we allow our calendars to consume our days to the point of not really doing anything with any gusto or fervor.

There are times when we *should* feast. There are times when we should pull out all the stops and celebrate with our beloved family and friends. Often that celebration includes great food and drink, but the most important element is the feast of our time and total presence to the people we love. A wonderful Lenten practice could be to have a special dinner and a good bottle of wine with a dear friend. But we also need the fasting. We need the time to be alone with the Lord. We need that quiet time to pray and sort out all the pieces of our lives.

Only when we learn to fast are we able to feast, and only feasting makes fasting special. Lent is a time to learn how to fast and how to feast. In the process we bring real passion back into our lives.

Isn't it a wonderful and holy moment when we have a special dinner and a bottle of wine with a dear friend?

## A Dead Girl and a Woman With a Hemorrhage

MATTHEW 9:18-26

*Monday of the Fourteenth Week of the Year*

"Please come and lay your hand on her and she will come back to life." Is there a more touching prayer in all of scripture than this one offered to Jesus by the synagogue leader whose little girl has just died?

How much this man loved his little girl! How deep and special is that beautiful bond between a daddy and his little princess. This father would have given or done anything to have his girl back. He would be willing to die himself if it meant her living.

We know we are on very holy ground when we are in the presence of such love. It is a love stronger than life and death itself. It is a love that gives us a hint of the love God has for us, his beloved children.

The most moving moments in my life have been those that brought me to the bedside of a sick or dying child. These moments are etched on my heart and have left such an impression on me that they have influenced who and what I am as a man and a priest. Being part of the overwhelming emotion of these moments has given me an experience I personally never had—that of being a loving parent. I was transported at these moments to a different world and a different life.

Love really *is* everything. Love is the closest we ever get to life and to God. Not to love is simply to exist, not really live. Not to love is to be dead and to be robbed of the meaning of life.

I remember so vividly the night Lauren died. She was surrounded by her mom and dad and adoring family. Lauren had spent six weeks in the hospital burn unit. When the night for her to go home arrived, we all knew it. Doctors and nurses came into the room. In their gowns it looked as if angels were filling the room preparing to take Lauren home.

The spirit of love touched each and every one of us and we prayed and wept. We all learned how to *really* pray the rosary in the preceding weeks. And now all was ready.

And so Jesus came and took Lauren's hand and said: "Arise, my love, my fair one, and come away; for now the winter is past, the rain is over and gone. The flowers appear on the earth. . . . Arise, my love, my fair one, and come away" (Song of Songs 2:10-13).

## The Healing of a Mute Man

MATTHEW 9:32-38

*Tuesday of the Fourteenth Week of the Year*

While the people proclaim the wonder of the deed of Jesus in casting out the demon from the mute man, the Pharisees are incapable of seeing the good and the wonder of the deed, and they make wild accusations against Jesus. The security of their lives and the validity of their ministry are called into question by this merciful and loving act of Jesus.

There is a message in this for us. Isn't it impossible sometimes to really listen to and honestly evaluate and appreciate what others are saying because they seem to be denying and questioning what we believe and what we do? It seems especially true for some church people who never really listen. Many of us are all ready to beat another down with our Bible or new Catechism because what another says will force us to critically look at our own premises. We don't like doing that because the structure of our belief might fall.

When our religious life is not centered in Christ, it becomes centered on and dependent upon a set of doctrinal formularies that become cold and lifeless, and are not really part of the experience of possessing the living God at all. When we begin to plumb the mystery of God, we soon begin to travel in areas that are unfamiliar to us. It is in taking the leap of faith that a whole new approach will demand of us that we begin to have an experience of God and God's glory in new and exciting ways.

It is so easy to follow the lead of the Pharisees and explain away the wonder of what we see with safe, shallow, and often untrue explanations. How much more exciting and fascinating it is to examine, test, and discuss new ideas and what brought them about.

## Sending Out the Twelve

MATTHEW 10:1-7

*Wednesday of the Fourteenth Week of the Year*

There is a triple action of Jesus toward the apostles: he calls them, he gives them authority, and he sends them out on a mission as *his* Twelve.

There is a disarming simplicity in the way Jesus walked into their lives and said: "Follow me." The amazing thing is that they did it. What an amazing thing Christ's call is! When you hear his voice, it's hard to forget it, at least completely. No matter where we wander and what we do, once he speaks to us we can never forget that voice! We may spend years running away and trying to distract ourselves, yet he's always there somewhere in the shadows. The lover never stops pursuing the beloved. Thompson described it so powerfully in *Hound of Heaven*. He waits so patiently. He never gives up, and ultimately he is never disappointed. Eventually we all say our "Yes!"

Why did Jesus call the Twelve? Why does Jesus call us? To answer that question is to begin to enter the heart of Jesus and the unique love he had for them and has for us. He calls those who need him most.

Jesus did not pick the holiest, most gifted, most talented, or even the nicest people in Galilee. He still doesn't pick the winners. He calls us. Why? Because he loves us in a special way, and he wants to share with us the depth of his heart and his love in a special way. Does it make you squirm to know that he called you even though so many people in your life are far more deserving? Good! It should! What should we do about it? Just say, "Thank you!" and do your best to respond to him in loving fidelity.

## The Mission of the Twelve

MATTHEW 10:7-15

*Thursday of the Fourteenth Week of the Year*

Jesus sends the twelve out with the exciting charge of announcing that the reign of God is at hand.

This is absolutely an exciting and special time. Jesus sends them out to begin a new age of fulfillment and hope. This reign of God will be marked by the curing of the sick, raising of the dead, healing of the lepers, and expelling of demons. This is a new day and a new age.

Jesus then tells his heralds of the new age not to worry about material and worldly things but to keep their hearts always fixed on the spiritual, the things of God.

Why is it that we have lost the excitement and the joy of proclamation? So much of our proclamation is so predictable. It is packaged in boxed parcels that are guaranteed to never interest, excite, or challenge anyone!

When Pope John XXIII opened Vatican II, didn't he have this sadness of the proclaimers in mind when he prayed for a New Pentecost? Didn't he pray that the Spirit would fill the church anew and that the ancient truths would be given a new form that would touch and excite the modern world?

As we begin this millennium, isn't this what is still needed? Don't we need parents, priests, sisters, lay ministers, and deacons to be filled with the power of God's love so that the church and world will be filled with new signs and wonders? Don't we need to see the sick cured, the dead raised, the lepers healed, and the demons cast out before our very eyes?

Of course we do! We will only see these signs and wonders when we fall in love with Love and when we allow the Holy Spirit to fill our hearts with the new wine and thus inebriate us in the joy of God's love.

This is what the new evangelization is. It is not new programs or theology or gimmicks or anything institutional. It is a humble and loving opening of our hearts to the God of surprise who has some wonderful gifts to give the world through the ministry of God's very incompetent, unworthy, and weak disciples, who at least have the brains to know that it is Jesus' church.

May this millennium be the time for us to give back the church to Jesus. May we begin to believe and trust that what he tells us in the gospel is what he really wants, and that the well-meaning and sincere religion we

have substituted for his heart is not really necessary—
only he is.

## Like Sheep Among Wolves

MATTHEW 10:16-23

*Friday of the Fourteenth Week of the Year*

Jesus continues his instructions as he sends the disciples out. He tells them and us to expect some very rough times. "I am sending you out like sheep among wolves. You must be clever as snakes and innocent as doves." He certainly asks us for an awful lot!

Jesus continues by promising trials, courts, and floggings. Then he says something that puts it all in its true context: "Do not worry about what you will say or how you will say it. You will be given what you are to say. You will not be the speakers; the Spirit of your Father will be speaking in you."

The disciple must be so close to the Lord that he or she lives in the Spirit of Jesus. When we are in constant union with the Spirit, we are given the words to say at every important juncture of our lives. Our prayerfulness is not the frantic prayer to the Holy Spirit of a student cramming for an exam in a subject he or she has neglected all semester. We never *cram*. We walk with the Lord each day. He leads us gently, and he is always there to guide and protect us. He never abandons us or leaves us as orphans. He is always with us.

As we hear the call of Jesus, as we are sent out to proclaim the reign, we can only give what we already possess. We possess the greatest of all gifts—the Lord Jesus. His Holy Spirit guides us at each and every moment, and he gives us the words to speak that will always confound his enemies.

All we can ever speak is truth and love. That will happen when we allow him to live in us. When we speak truth and love, no one can ever hurt us and we can *really* never hurt another person. When we speak truth and love, Christ is present and no one can ever conquer him.

## Courage Under Persecution

MATTHEW 10:24-33

*Saturday of the Fourteenth Week of the Year*

Jesus continues the theme of living in his truth and love. He stresses that we must be like him. We cannot expect that the students will be treated better than he, who is the Teacher, or a slave better than the master. Not only must we expect and embrace all that was done to Jesus; we must embrace the kind of ministry that Jesus embraced. He went to the poor, the ignorant, and the non-religious. He called people who had nothing but faith.

Why are we so surprised that the same is required of us? Why do we balk and complain when we find so many of our people unevangelized and hungry for anything of the Spirit? For some reason we expect and want a super church where everyone is well groomed and where everyone knows the ecclesiastical ropes.

It is so sad to see the church treat people in a condescending manner. When you read the rule books of parishes for people trying to have their children baptized and receive first communion, what comes across is a subtle but real anger toward the unwashed and uninvolved. We seem to want a very nice and cozy little community that knows the rules and pays their way. The people that Jesus sought out don't seem to belong here at all, and sometimes Jesus doesn't seem to fit either.

Jesus is the model of ministry. Jesus opens his arms and embraces all. Jesus welcomes sinners and even eats with them. Jesus doesn't turn people away; he welcomes.

125

Jesus' name becomes associated with the most disreputable people. Jesus will talk to and eat with anyone.

The eucharist continues this table ministry of Jesus where everyone has a place and everyone is welcome. The parish church and the Sunday eucharist become the most exciting place on earth because all the misfits are there by special invitation of the Lord Jesus himself.

Jesus promises us that when we allow him to guide us in our ministry he will always be there for us. He loves us so much, and he will always take care of us. When we treat his little ones with compassion, he will never cease to love us and treat us in the same way. Jesus tells us again not to be afraid.

## The Cost of Discipleship

### MATTHEW 10:34–11:1

*Monday of the Fifteenth Week of the Year*

One of the few blessings that emerged from the Nazi insanity of the Second World War was the writings of the Protestant pastor, Dietrich Bonhoeffer. His book *The Cost of Discipleship* makes a beautiful commentary on today's gospel. Jesus teaches us today that the gospel will not always bring us peace; it may also be the cause of persecution, misunderstanding, and, as in the case of both Jesus and Bonhoeffer, death itself. Grace is not always cheap or easy. There is a price to pay for being a disciple of Jesus.

When we look at the history of the church in our own lifetime, we see almost a return to the brutality of the persecutions of the early church. We have seen in our own times an archbishop murdered as he said Mass. We have seen the horror of the rape and murder of the sisters along with the murder of the Jesuits—all in that tortured country of El Salvador. The soil of that country has been made red in the loving deaths of thousands of innocent compesinos.

Today the follower of Jesus is often asked to give up a lot of the culture and values of society to walk with Jesus. What is acceptable to the world is not always acceptable to us. Making as much money as you can and accumulating as many things as possible are not our goals. Living in peace and love with our God and ourselves is what we seek in our lives and endeavors.

It's not easy living in a society where abortion, premarital sex, and marital infidelity are accepted as normal and even good. How difficult it is for the young person to make choices that are contrary to the norms of our society and what "everybody else is doing."

While we all must take up our cross each day and follow Jesus, it does become a lot easier when there is a community of sisters and brothers who are there to support, encourage, and, when need be, challenge us. That is what church is meant to be. That is what family is meant to be. When we live in that community of love we have the ability to face and to do anything. We do it with the Lord Jesus and with the church. We don't stand alone.

## Reproaches to Unrepentant Towns

MATTHEW 11:20-24

*Tuesday of the Fifteenth Week of the Year*

Today, Jesus reproaches the two towns of Chorazin and Bethsaida. He does so because they have been the scenes of Jesus working miracles of grace and love in abundance. Indeed, Jesus has worked most of his miracles in these villages, and there has not been a noticeable change of heart or conversion among the people. Jesus goes so far as to say that if Tyre and Sidon had experienced his ministry, they would have repented in sack cloth and ashes. Even Capernaum does not escape the condemnation of Jesus.

I think of this gospel today in terms of my own life and my inadequate response to the graces that Jesus has lavished upon me. When I think of the family, education, friends, opportunities, and mostly of the love that the Lord has lavished upon me, I feel a lot like Chorazin and Bethsaida! So much has been given and so little has been returned.

This gospel is a reality check for us today. Today the Lord afflicts us with the truth of the gifts that he has given to us, and he asks us to reflect upon what we have done with those gifts. Our reflection is not meant to condemn us for past failures but to inspire us to begin again. All of Christianity seems to center around the gift of hope. Even if we have failed and not given anywhere near our best, the Lord invites us to take his hand and begin again.

We have a Savior Jesus in whom there is always hope and possibility. It is the joy of our God to allow him to find us. When this happens, there is more joy in heaven—in God—than there would be in all of our hearts combined. Our well-being, joy, peace, fulfillment, and happiness delights our God. God loves us so much that it brings him untold joy for us to allow him to find us and help us.

Jesus calls us today to realism and to hope—realism in being honest in what we have done and hope in knowing that we are not condemned and that we have another chance to begin and to live the life that Jesus wants us to enjoy. Remember, every saint has a past and every sinner has a future in Christ Jesus.

# The Wisdom of Children

*Wednesday of the Fifteenth Week of the Year*

Jesus tells us today that what the Father has hidden from the clever and the learned he has revealed to the merest children. Jesus is talking about the childlike quality that is always present in the true believer. He is not talking about being childish or immature, but he is speaking about being childlike. This childlike quality is expected when he tells us to be innocent as doves but wise as serpents.

What is it to be childlike? It has all to do with the heart. It is the quality of the person who has seen it all but remains basically innocent. It is the quality of wonder, excitement, anticipation, enjoyment, and joy that truly happy people seem to possess. The most learned and gifted people can be very childlike. They somehow seem never to lose the wisdom of looking upon all things as gifts. The simplest things—from the smell of fresh brewed coffee to watching a beautiful sunset—please and delight the childlike.

The childlike disciple of Jesus is not childish. He or she is not immature, scatter-brained, or impractical. The childlike person knows the price of love, commitment, and fidelity. He or she knows how to get things done without ever compromising principles or values. This person confounds the powerful and unscrupulous because he or she lives by truth alone. They say what they mean and they mean what they say.

There is a process of becoming childlike. It consists of going back to hard questions about how we reverence and cherish people, ourselves, and God's creation. It consists of repeatedly asking ourselves the question that our youth brings to our attention more and more: "What would Jesus do?" How did Jesus treat people? How did he celebrate life? How did he use power and fame?

The journey to being childlike is well worth the trip. When we become like little children, then we can really accept and rejoice at being children in the arms of the beloved Parent. We can really celebrate the joy of being so loved and cherished by God who loves us so much and delights to hold us close.

## Rest for the Weary

MATTHEW 11:28-30

*Thursday of the Fifteenth Week of the Year*

"Come to me." These beautiful and consoling words of Jesus are among the most touching in all of scripture. If we really want to understand their depth, we have to think of ourselves in our most terrible moments—moments when we thought that we could not go on. These were times of deep depression; terrible sickness, our own or that of loved ones; dreadful family problems; or even the death of a family member. Perhaps the experience of mental illness was that "moment of hell."

Whatever it was, we have all gone through moments like these. We have all experienced them, and we have all held a loved one who has gone through them. The abandonment that Jesus suffered in the Garden of Gethsemane and on the cross is part and parcel of everyone's life.

These moments are also tremendous moments of grace. They are the opportunity for us to allow God to love us and help us. God calls to us to come to him always, but especially when we are powerless and need him most. Fr. Henri Nouwen in his book *The Return of the Prodigal Son* has a beautiful section about how happy we make our loving Father when we come home to him. Isn't it a wonderful thing when we hear his voice calling us and we respond? Shouldn't we also make God happy by allowing him to show us his love? Don't parents most cherish the moments when they have rescued their children from real or imagined danger and held them safely in their arms? The delight and joy of our God is without limit when we come home and allow him to hold us and cherish us in his arms.

"Come to me, all you who are weary and find life burdensome, and I will refresh you. Take my yoke upon your shoulders and learn from me, for I am gentle and humble of heart. Your souls will find rest, for my yoke is easy and my burden light."

The temptation will be to think that we don't deserve God's love. Where was I when things were going well? Why didn't I go to God when everything was so great? I only go to God when I need God.

Of course we are not worthy of God's love. Of course we don't deserve God, and yet God loves us just the same unconditionally and completely. God's love has no limit. God loves us forever, especially when we don't deserve it. Why not make our God happy by allowing him to hold us in his arms today and love us?

## Picking Grain on the Sabbath

MATTHEW 12:1-8

*Friday of the Fifteenth Week of the Year*

"The Son of Man is the Lord of the sabbath." What is Jesus up to? Revolution, plain and simple! Jesus is changing all the rules. At the heart of this new way is the obvious principle that people are more important than things and rules. For Jesus it is not breaking the law to do "work" on the sabbath or for hungry men to take the grain from the stalks and eat it. It was also not against the law for the hungry soldiers of King David to enter the Temple and eat the holy bread that was part of the

Temple's liturgical worship. Let there be no question about it—it was a very big deal for the scribes and Pharisees who saw it. They thought it was sinful and sacrilegious, and they thought that this Jesus was "off the wall," if not a sinner, in suggesting that David and his men along with Jesus and his disciples did a good thing.

Simple hunger seemed to be more important to Jesus than centuries of religious practice and custom. In this we see the dilemma and problem that will eventually lead Jesus to the cross. He habitually breaks the law. Whether it is taking the grain from the stalks on the sabbath or eating regularly with sinners, Jesus is saying that the Lord has great limitations and that other values mean more than the law. The need of a suffering person or a sinner always has priority.

The dilemma of Jesus will always be the dilemma of those who follow him. As the church and society institutionalize Jesus and the gospel, his true followers will always be in conflict with the letter of the law because they will be attempting to discern what Jesus would want of them here and now. The institution will always (just like the Pharisees) demand total obedience to the letter of the law. The one part of the church will try to preserve while another will try to adapt.

For the most part, we will try to see where the Lord's Spirit is leading. We obey, but we also think and discern and seek the truth. We cherish the tradition, but we also know that the Lord never ceases to speak to us and we must ultimately be obedient to the prompting of the Holy Spirit in a well-formed conscience.

Unfortunately, there are still crucifixions in the community of love, which is his holy church. The church itself, which is you and me, must hear and understand the words of Jesus: "It is mercy I desire and not sacrifice."

# God's Chosen Servant

## MATTHEW 12:14-21

*Saturday of the Fifteenth Week of the Year*

The Suffering Servant of the Book of Isaiah is at the center of Jesus' message today. Jesus uses these beautiful images to describe himself, the church, and his disciples. They are moving words that stress the humility of Jesus as the Servant leader who has come not to be served but to serve and to give his life as a ransom for the many.

Jesus tells us that like him, we are the chosen servants in whom God delights. God delights in us. He loves us so much. He calls us by name to continue this servant ministry of Jesus. The servant Jesus is the foot washer, the humble one who takes the lowest place so that he might serve the poor. This church of Jesus is the place of humility, service, and compassion, not the place of force, power, or condemnation. The servant church embraces and loves the world and gives witness to the following of Jesus and this gospel by the humble and loving example of who Jesus is and what he means. That teaching by humble example is more powerful than all the words that can ever be written or spoken.

Jesus and we, his disciples, are anointed in the Holy Spirit. Isaiah tells us that we are to proclaim justice to the world, not charity. The greatest moments in the life of the modern church have been those in which our church and pope have proclaimed justice for the poor. The shedding of the blood of Oscar Romero, the Central American Jesuits, the church women of El Salvador, and the thousands of innocent compesinos proclaim the gospel with an authority that literally deafens the world.

The Suffering Servant touches and heals in his gentleness and tenderness. "The bruised reed he will not crush." "The smoldering wick he will not quench." "In his name people will find hope."

What a demanding and seemingly impossible role Jesus calls his disciples to! Can we ever achieve it? Of course not! But that doesn't mean that we don't keep on trying. We never give up and we never stop. We try to be open to the unending call that Jesus gives us—to imitate him as the Suffering and Humble Servant.

May the Holy Spirit continue to encourage us and give us hope that we will become like Jesus and be the Suffering Servant.

## The Sign of Jonah

### MATTHEW 12:38-42

*Monday of the Sixteenth Week of the Year*

"Teacher, we want to see you work some signs!" So do we. We all love the extraordinary. We delight in the dramatic effects of a Cecil B. DeMille movie. We all want the fireworks and the marvelous. But it doesn't happen that way at all. Jesus is too ordinary, too human for any of that.

It's incredible how much energy is put forth into finding the apparition that's just perfect, the prayer that says it all, or the devotion with the guarantee of answering our prayers. We want the miraculous and the spectacular and Jesus will give us only the ordinary and the humdrum.

Jesus gives us three daily, powerful, but very ordinary miracles. He gives us community, the word of God, and the eucharist. It is in finding the real meaning in our lives of these three miracles that we find him and so find everything.

We find Jesus in community. It is in relationships that we touch the living God. Relationships mean people, and they mean love and commitment. The more we grow in relationships, the more we find God. In loving and being loved we are at the very threshold of holding, possessing, and knowing God. If we want to really know who God is we must grow in knowledge and love of one another.

We find Jesus in his living word. As we learn to allow Jesus to speak and to touch us, we grow in his life. The scriptures are a love letter from Jesus to us. To learn how to read that letter in gentle faith transforms our hearts, turning them from hearts of stone to hearts of flesh. The word is the gentle rain that soaks the very being of our souls, preparing them to give faith the good harvest. As we allow Jesus to speak to us in the word at Mass or private prayer, we become the new creation.

We find Jesus in the eucharist. What a miracle it is that we are privileged to receive the very life of Jesus in this holy sacrament. He comes to us to fill us with his love. In the holy moment of communion he gives us all that he is. How great is the love of Jesus! How powerful is his love for us. What miracles happen when we recognize him in the breaking of the bread.

Jesus gives us three great signs: community, word, and eucharist. We don't need any others.

## The Family of Jesus

MATTHEW 12:46-50

*Tuesday of the Sixteenth Week of the Year*

This gospel tends to make me a little uncomfortable. "Your mother and your brothers are standing out there and they wish to speak to you." Instead of saying something to the effect of being happy to see his mother, Jesus seems to brush her aside and be almost rude to her. I would love to see Jesus be more of the loving and devoted Son that he was.

Jesus is teaching a profound lesson. He is teaching that being a member of the Kingdom is far greater than any earthly bond, even that of mother and son, even that of Mary and Jesus. Not only that, but Mary and her role can only be understood and appreciated in terms of the meaning of the church. Mary is not outside of or apart from the church. She is a member of the body of believers.

What begins as a seeming "put down" of Mary actually leads us to a far deeper and more beautiful understanding of Mary as the woman of faith, totally identified with and related to all of her children. When we see Mary in this light we see her as being part and parcel of our own life and struggle. She ceases to be the plastic saint and becomes the living Mother who is also our sister and who shares in all the joy and pain of being a human being as we journey through all the ups and downs of life.

This thinking opens up all kinds of new understandings of Mary. We go beyond the safe and traditional titles of Mary in her glory. As beautiful and consoling as they might be, they tell only half of her story.

Mary's "Magnificat" leads us into the heart of the "little one" of God who is sister to all of us. This Mary is the mother of a man who is executed, she is the poor woman, she is the disenfranchised, she is the shunned and despised one at the foot of the cross. She is the sorrowful mother whose heart is broken because they have killed her Son.

Mary is part of the family. She is there to gather us together and to comfort and console us. She belongs to us because she is one of us. She is the little one who will declare: "All generations shall call me blessed for he who is mighty has done great things for me!"

# The Parable of the Sower

### MATTHEW 13:1-9

*Wednesday of the Sixteenth Week of the Year*

What a great picture today's gospel presents: Jesus sits by the side of the sea. Today's gospel takes place during the summer when most of us, like Jesus, go to sit by the side of the sea. One of the most wonderful and life-giving experiences for me is to sit at the beach on these beautiful days and marvel at the beauty of the world God has given to us. The hot sun, the cold salt water, the ocean breeze–my God, how magnificent! No lunch is as delicious as one enjoyed by the sea! No conversation as interesting as one by the sea! No book is as enjoyable as one perused by the sea!

Jesus is giving us an example when he sits on the beach. He is telling us to put down the Bible once in a while and to read the book of creation—his creation. Frequently we scoff at the comments of so many, especially the young, that they find God in nature, at the beach, or at the mountains. Unfortunately, they offer it as an explanation of why they don't go to church. They don't need organized religion because they have found God in nature, they say. Pastorally, we try to lead them in love from his creation to his word, to his family, and to his body and blood.

But our beautiful young people may also lead us closer to God by helping us to use God's magnificent creation as our first and basic prayer book. There is a presence of God at the beach, on the water, at sunrise or sunset, in the mountains and in the desert, in the ice, cold, snow, rain, and heat that is profound and life-giving. Not to read this book makes us far less capable of understanding and appreciating the glory and majesty of our God.

The magnificence of the psalms, the natural references of the Hebrew scriptures, the agricultural and natural references of Jesus, like today's story of the sower, take on a whole different meaning to the holy ones who find their God in nature.

The revival of Celtic spirituality has been a wonderful source of returning to nature and its author. It is teaching us how to pray with nature, seasons, light and darkness, and our beautiful bodies. It is another blow to the distrust of the physical and material that perjures the church.

Our ancient liturgies were so much more in tune with nature and its cycles than we are. The Easter Vigil (before the liturgists cleaned it up) was one of the most sensuous and earthy acts of worship. It truly used all nature—from fire to anointing naked bodies—to glorify this magnificent God of creation and God's wonderful world.

Let's sit with Jesus at the beach and smell, listen, look, and touch the book of his love. Let's also take a nature walk to continue a walk of praise:

## A WALK OF THANKSGIVING

I walk in thanksgiving
    for the sunlit years of childhood
    for tall trees and dewy morning grass
    for warm winds and singing birds and yellow
        flower cups
    for laughter and discovery and the gift of wonder . . .
And because I walk in thanksgiving, I walk in belief.

I walk in thanksgiving
    for the years of growing awareness of life
    of a world peopled with life and alive with people
    of my own self as one among many selves
    fashioning myself through reaching out and up;
    for the experience of growth through uncertainty,
    the risk of life, of love, of liberty . . .
And because I walk in thanksgiving, I walk in trust.

I walk in thanksgiving
    for friendship and insight and the gift of prayer
    for windy nights and sunsplit waves
    for the splendor of autumn on rocky peaks
        gold on green, and flame against blue,
    for music and balloons and the song of the world
    for the intensity of life, for challenge and delight . . .
And because I walk in thanksgiving, I walk in joy.

I walk in thanksgiving
    for life that comes, not as a whole, but in little
        pieces called people;
    for tenderness and strength, for gentleness and
        warmth
    for weakness and pain, for anguish and ambiguity
    for laughter and courage and the gift of friends
    for the risk of life and the risk of God . . .
And because I walk in thanksgiving, I walk in love.

I walk in thanksgiving for faith and hope and joy and
    love
And because I walk in thanksgiving, I walk in God.

Author unknown

## The Purpose of Parables

MATTHEW 13:10-17

*Thursday of the Sixteenth Week of the Year*

Today, Jesus is asked a question that I bet you've been dying to ask him. I know I have. "Why do you use stories to teach?" In some ways I used to think that the style of the parables was a bit "hokey" or simplistic. Why doesn't the Son of God simply teach and preach the message? Why does he have to complicate it with these stories, touching as they may be?

I came to the answer to these questions only after years of preaching myself. I began to discover that most of my preaching that was theoretical and heady had very little real impact on my people. It was only after I began to tell a story that my preaching began to have an effect, or at least began to be real. It's not really hard to understand why this is so.

The preaching of Jesus is about real life occurrences. Some of them really happened and some of them were made up in a rabbinical style. Jesus was a rabbi. His style was to clothe the message (himself) in a form that would be remembered and easily repeated.

The best intentioned preacher or teacher may believe completely in the message and think that simply because it is the truth all you have to do is tell it. After all, doesn't the truth make you free? Well, yes and no.

The truth has got to be packaged in such a way that people can grab on to it. One could read the new Catechism and the Documents of Vatican II and never be touched by that experience. In fact, they are a known cure for insomnia. The message has to be part of a story, my story, my hearer's story . . . somebody's story.

In the parables of Jesus the pious sayings are few; the life experience stories are many. They are above and below us at the same time. They are obvious and mysterious. They always leave you looking for more. They are always short and to the point, never belaboring the point. They are never finished. That's up to the hearer to do. They are personal and they are true because they talk about life, people, experience, and nature.

As we preach the message of Jesus, whether we are parent or teacher, the context or story will do more than the content. How we present the message is as critical as the message itself. We are the medium that contains the message. We in fact become the message itself as we try to incarnate all that Jesus is and all that Jesus teaches.

# The Parable of the Sower Explained

## MATTHEW 13:18-23

*Friday of the Sixteenth Week of the Year*

Jesus proceeds to explain the parable of the sower because there is always a mysterious aspect to a parable; no parable is ever totally clear. There is a dimension of the unfinished story in every seemingly finished story.

The heart is represented by the different types of soil in this parable. What kind of soil does your heart represent? Is your heart the path, the rocky ground, the thorns, or the good soil?

I guess we are different at different times and moments in our lives. One thing is clear: we can only accept the seed (word) according to our disposition—the condition of the soil of our hearts.

Our process of conversion is to work to prepare our soil (heart) to receive the seed (word) so that it may take root and bring forth faith in abundance. Is there anything concrete that the Spirit is leading you to do as you hear the words of the parable? What must be done so that the soil is ready and prepared to embrace the seed and bring forth the abundant fruit?

We can never cease our task of preparing our hearts to receive God's love. The tilling, watering, and maintaining of the soil never ceases. We are never finished in our process of becoming ready to receive the word in our hearts and allowing it to take root and bring forth fruit.

The consoling thing is that our God never stops sowing the seed. God doesn't do it only once. God doesn't give up if it falls among the thorns. No, our God sows the seed over and over again. God never gives up on us and never casts us aside. God's mercy and love know no limits. Our God has unending patience and understanding. God rejoices at those beautiful times when the seed reaches at least some good soil that is ready to do some work for God.

## The Parable of the Weeds Among the Wheat

MATTHEW 13:24-30

*Saturday of the Sixteenth Week of the Year*

The parable of the wheat and the weed is the story of every man and every woman. It is the story of humanity. Our souls are beautiful gardens in which many beautiful flowers grow, but next to these flowers grow seven kinds of weeds. Their names are: pride, covetousness, lust, anger, envy, gluttony, and sloth. The presence of these weeds drives good people crazy! Why does God allow these weeds to grow alongside the beautiful flowers? Why doesn't God just rip them out and give us some peace?

The answer is because God can't. God can't because if he did it would destroy the beauty of who and what we are. The seeds and the wheat grow from something very deep in us, like our psychological or spiritual DNA. The weeds and the wheat are entwined and interrelated. If we were to rip out the weeds we would do immeasurable damage to who we are. We would be destroyed.

There is another path. There is another side to the weeds that needs to be cultivated. We must go back to the essence of what the weed is and begin to cultivate its positive and life-giving side.

Pride converted becomes good self-esteem and a healthy self-image. Covetousness converted can become a proper appreciation of created things along with their correct use. Lust can become deep and tender love and the cherishing rather than using of another. Anger instead of being neurotic and destructive can become the pursuit of justice for oneself and others. Envy can become the appreciation of another's gift and the challenge to become one's best. Gluttony can lead us to the gift of community and celebration and the proper use of all gifts to praise God. Sloth can lead us to appreciate the moment and to the gift of reflection and tranquility.

So, perhaps a better prayer than asking for the weeds to be ripped out is to allow the weed to lead us to its core so that it many begin to grow in a new and life-giving way. It is then that the wheat of God's presence and love will come forth.

The demons will never go away. The weeds will always be there. No matter how fast you pull them out, they will grow back. That's what makes us so beautiful. We're human.

## The Parables of the Mustard Seed and the Yeast

MATTHEW 13:31-35

*Monday of the Seventeenth Week of the Year*

Jesus gives us two images today of the reign of God and of the gift of faith: the mustard seed and yeast kneaded into flour. He again speaks in the homey examples that his friends and neighbors can understand: the garden and the kitchen. For starters, Jesus is telling us that we don't have far to look if we want to find him and his message. We find him in everything, every situation, and every human relationship. We don't have to go far to touch our God. God is truly around us, in us, and for us in all things.

The image of the mustard seed tells us about the power of faith and its ability to change our lives and the lives of countless generations. I see this unfold before me each day in the faith and lives of simple and humble people, especially parents. As they share their beautiful faith with their children, co-workers, and friends, miracles happen. We are never the same after having been in the presence of people of deep faith. Their way of living and looking at things forces us to look at our own lives, our values, and our future. People who help us to find the tiny mustard seed of faith introduce us to a treasure that will direct our whole existence. That tiny seed grows and a magnificent tree of faith grows for ourselves and all those in our lives to take shelter and be protected against the storms.

As we grow in faith we become the anchor that our friends come to rely upon. They in turn find their little mustard seed as we did. They plant it, and before we know it there is a forest of faith that we call the community, the church.

We are also called to be like the yeast, that mysterious and marvelous substance that brings life to the dough and causes it to rise. So, too, do we bring true life into the world as we allow the power of Christ to live in us and to bring life to all around us.

If there is one thing about faith, it is *alive*. Nothing can stay the same when it is touched by God's love. Neither can we be the same when the finger of God's love touches us and calls us to share that life in the world.

## The Parable of the Weeds Explained

MATTHEW 13:35-43

*Tuesday of the Seventeenth Week of the Year*

Jesus speaks today about the harvest at the end of the world. He speaks about the judgment in the image of the gathering and burning of the weeds and the gathering of the good harvest into the Kingdom of God.

It's a healthy thing for us to pause once in a while and reflect upon the end of the world, the judgment, heaven and hell. We never want to do this in a morbid way and never want to forget the mercy and love of God and how this great mercy sustains us and encourages us never to lose heart. We do, however, need to look at our journey to the Lord.

As the Lord calls us and invites us to become more and more like him, we realize that it is a process and a journey. We do not become who and what we were meant to be immediately. In all of our lives there is struggle, success, and failure. We never reach the place where we should be, but we also never stop trying or moving to what the Lord would like to see us become.

The Christian life is a struggle. We become the beautiful harvest of love not because we have achieved all the virtues, but because we never give up the struggle. To be faithful to the struggle is to be faithful to Jesus. To begin again each day, even after yesterday's seeming failure, is the process of our faith in the Lord Jesus and the power of his grace.

This garden of the saints that Jesus tends is indeed a motley group. There are many black eyes, bruises, and limps among the elect in the garden. There are many weeds that are a part of and growing with the blossoms of his love. The blossoms are like a trimmed group of people who keep trying to get it right but never totally succeed. But they don't give up.

At the day of judgment perhaps Jesus will ask to see our hands. As we open them he will see how bruised and torn they are. Jesus will see in them the struggles we've had each day of our lives. He will see our victories, but he will also rejoice at our wounds and failures because they are the impetus to put our faith in him and begin again. He will smile and say to us, "Well done, my good and faithful servant. Enter now into the joy of your Master."

# The Parables of the
# Hidden Treasure and the Pearl

### MATTHEW 13:44-46

*Wednesday of the Seventeenth Week of the Year*

The treasure in the field and the pearl of great price are the two beautiful examples of the Kingdom of heaven that Jesus uses in today's gospel.

In both cases the person in the gospel realizes the value of both of these things and goes out and sells everything to purchase the field and to purchase the pearl. It is well worth whatever he has to give up to obtain the field with its treasure or the pearl of great price.

It leads us to think about our real treasure and our pearl of great price. As someone observes our life, what would they say is our "treasure" and our "pearl"? What would they say that we are living for and working for?

Let us pray that our hard work and effort flows from a passionate and powerful love that we have for the Lord, for our families and friends, and for Christ's poor. Let us not be working for *things*, let us be working for relationships of love.

I know many wonderful and holy people who don't believe that they are spiritual because they're working for so many hours, or even a second job. They will complain that they have no time to pray during the day or go to church activities in the evening. Why are they working so hard—because they're raising children and paying college tuition. Their whole activity and work is directed to their home and caring for their children and giving them the best they can.

These good people have found the treasure—their children and their home. Instead of giving these holy people guilt trips because they work so hard, wouldn't it be healthier if the church helped them to see that all they do is holy? Wouldn't it make more sense to help them see

146

that their labor is prayer and to teach them ways to formally turn this all over to the Lord as their prayer of love?

Our people look to the church for help in how to keep their homes, marriages, and children centered on Christ in the midst of hectic activity and work for their families. What a sad thing when they are given the impressions that they are "worldly" or "materialistic," often by some people who wouldn't have a clue about the sacrifice and labor these holy people put into finding their "treasure" and their "pearl."

## The Parable of the Net

MATTHEW 13:47-53

*Thursday of the Seventeenth Week of the Year*

What a beautiful image Jesus gives us of the church! The net! The net is thrown into the sea and collects every kind of fish. Look at the net. Look at your parish church on Sunday morning. It is filled with every kind of "fish." There we are—every size, shape, texture, color, and variety. We even have our own special "odor." Each fish is so special and so unique, and we all belong in the net of Christ's love.

Jesus welcomes everyone. Everyone has a special place in the net of his love. The common denominator is our humanity. What a motley but beautiful group we are in the net. We are rich and poor, young and old, educated and unlettered, gay and straight, married and single, widowed and divorced, happily and not so happily married, priest, sister, and deacon. We are everybody. We are the world.

The incredible thing about this church, this net, is that everyone belongs. *I* belong. *We* belong. Our God has loved us so totally and completely. God has called us into being and has sent Jesus to be our brother and friend. He lovingly welcomes me to sit at his side in the meal of his love—the eucharist. This net is my home and my family. The more I love my sisters and brothers in the net the more I am loved and the deeper my peace and joy become as a member of this family.

At the end of the world, God will separate the good from the bad. Remember, only God will be Judge! We don't have that right or privilege. We don't take it upon ourselves to be God. Only the Lord will be the judge. This merciful and loving Father who sees our hearts will judge us in perfect love and merciful justice. I think at the judgment many that were judged as "bad" will turn out to be the most beautiful fish in the net, and many who seemed or pretended to be so wonderful will be saved only through the merciful love of God.

In the meantime, enjoy yourself in the net. The church is the most wonderful and crazy place you can ever be. The door is never closed and so the place is filled with wild and crazy people just like you and me!

## The Rejection at Nazareth

MATTHEW 13:54-58

*Friday of the Seventeenth Week of the Year*

Today Jesus experiences rejection. His townspeople turn on him and turn off their ears and hearts to his message because they know him and his family too well. What they are really saying is "Who does he think he is?" The result of their disbelief was the inability of Jesus to perform many miracles there because of their lack of faith.

It becomes a problem for us too. Sometimes we can't cope with the teaching and the wisdom of someone we know or someone who is close to us. Their humanity and their ordinariness prevent us from accepting and being open to them. Priests are the worst for this. We really don't like to see, let alone support, another priest who is gifted and has a following. After all, we were with him in the seminary. "Who does he think he is?" "He's no better than we are!"

It takes a very humble heart to hear a message and let it touch our hearts. We put all kinds of blocks and obstacles to the word being taught and preached. We can dismiss the message because we don't like the one presenting it. We can write it off because the bearer of the message is too sophisticated or too common. We can dismiss the message because we rationalize it or say it doesn't apply to us.

It does us good to reflect upon all the people in our lives whom we dismiss for many reasons because of our own limitations and our personal prejudice. It can be a spouse or the pope or our friends whom we dismiss and ignore because we don't like the message.

Sometimes the closer we are to the church, the more inhibited is our ability to hear the word. We simply dismiss the liberal, the conservative, the Right to Life person, the peace and justice person—anyone who is not on our wavelength. God forbid that we ever think that the Jew, Protestant, or Moslem has something to teach.

The God of truth speaks through all people of faith and love. The more we are willing to listen and learn, the more the truth of Jesus can grow in our hearts. Jesus was dismissed in Nazareth and he is still dismissed because we don't like the people who bear his message.

## The Death of John the Baptist

MATTHEW 14:1-12

*Saturday of the Seventeenth Week of the Year*

This is such a troubling and sad gospel. The execution of John the Baptist is so brutal and so evil. Today, in a country where men and women are executed, the gospel reminds us of our ethic of life. We must not take the life of a holy prophet or the life of a serial killer. They are both precious in God's sight. "Thou shalt not kill" shouts at us as we choose death over life in capital punishment, abortion, poverty, and war. Our consistent ethic of life calls us to reverence and respect the rights of every person. It calls us to justice.

Perhaps the saddest part of the gospel story is the relationship between Herodias and her daughter. The mother encourages her daughter to do an erotic dance for Herod and his drinking buddies. So little has changed from then to now. What a heartbreak it is when a parent leads a child astray and is not the parent they should be for their children. And then comes the sin beyond all sins: "Ask for the head of John the Baptist." And she does. There are few moments in the whole of the Bible worse than this one. The story of Herodias rivals even that of David in his lust for Bathsheba that leads him to murder.

In the midst of this scene is Herod. Herod knew that John was a holy prophet. He was attracted by his words. If John had gotten through to him, he might have had a different place in history.

Herod is so taken by the sensuous Salome that with the several drinks under his belt he promises her under oath, "I'll give you anything you want, just ask me." His buddies are delighted. After spiritual direction from mom, Salome makes her request: "I want you to give me, at once, the head of John the Baptist on a platter." She gets her request and gives it to her mother: "Happy Mother's Day!"

Poor Herod, he really doesn't want to do this. Even he knows how evil this is. But the old demon of ego gets to him. "What will the boys think if I renege?" I wonder if Herod ever slept again. I wonder how much wine he had to consume each day to forget, at least for a while, his terrible sin.

Herod is a lot like us. He knows what is right, but he can't do it. He has sold out in so many ways that when the great test comes along he is powerless. Perhaps as we try to find meaning in the Herod story we might look at our own story. If we say "no" to the Lord in many little ways but promise to be faithful in the big things, we deceive ourselves. Virtue is not doing the big things for God, but rather doing the little things daily. Each day we have the opportunity to say "yes" to the Lord in so many ways. Let's not miss a single opportunity. *(See also Mark 6:14-29.)*

## Feeding of the Five Thousand

### MATTHEW 14:13-21

*Monday of the Eighteenth Week of the Year*

Today's gospel begins with Jesus hearing the news that John the Baptist is dead. Jesus has to be by himself to process this news of his beloved cousin's death and to weep and mourn as he prays for him. Jesus is not immune to the pain of losing someone he loves. Tradition tells us that he was there when St. Joseph died. He broke down in tears at the death of his friend Lazarus. Jesus didn't play-act in human situations, he lived them. As painful as most deaths were for Jesus, the death of John was the worst. John the Baptist was murdered. His death was the result of pride, lust, ignorance, and vanity.

The death of a martyr—from John to the martyrs in El Salvador—is precious in God's eyes because it is such a gift of love when someone gives their very life for their God and their flock. Gift of God or not, this murder breaks Jesus' heart. The one of whom Jesus said no man born of woman was greater than, John the Baptist, was hacked to death; and Jesus must deal with his anger and hurt and maybe even lack of faith, just as we do when we are overwhelmed by the seeming history of hate over love. Yet in the blood of John and Oscar Romero and others, a new and greater community takes over. Love does conquer all.

Jesus doesn't have much time to be alone. The crowds follow him. They are so hungry for his word, but they are also hungry for some bread. The day grows later and the hunger pains become real.

The disciples are all for sending the crowds home. After all, they have only five loaves and a couple of fish. That's nothing. They have nothing to feed this crowd.

But Jesus, in this prelude to the eucharist, takes the loaves and the fishes in his hands. He blesses, breaks, and distributes this holy food, and the crowds are satisfied with twelve baskets left over.

Miracles happen when we place our lives in the hands of Jesus. We may think that we have, or are, nothing; yet, when we learn to trust him and truly believe that he leads us and guides us, there is no limit to what we can accomplish and do in his power.

So many Christians are afraid of failure. They never try to do anything new because they may fail and be embarrassed. It is so much easier just to do what you *have* to do, then you can sit back and find fault with those who will take a chance and are not afraid to make a mistake.

When we place it all in the hands of Jesus and let him do a little of the worrying, life is so much more fun. Not only do we succeed, but also, we find ourselves with twelve baskets left over.

# Jesus on the Water

MATTHEW 14:22-36

*Tuesday of the Eighteenth Week of the Year*

In today's gospel, we find Jesus alone and at prayer. He sends the disciples away to precede him in their boat to the other side of the lake.

Jesus alone and at prayer is a scene that fills us with all kinds of thoughts. How did Jesus pray? What was it like when he opened his heart to his beloved Father and was totally present to him? I don't think Jesus needed a lot of words in moments like this. I think he prayed in the Spirit of love and faith by surrendering himself completely to the holy will of his Father. He prayed that he would be and do all that the Father wished. Certainly, there were times of prayer when Jesus used words; times when he was broken and reached out for help and consolation. This was a time when he was all alone and all he wanted was to be with his Father, simply to enjoy the peace, joy, and love of being held by the One who loved him most.

The model of the contemplative prayer of Jesus, the prayer of the heart, the wordless simple prayer of love, is one for us to imitate. After all, the same Spirit of love who prayed in Jesus is the Spirit we have received and who prays in us. What is more powerful and meaningful for us than to be totally present to our God so that God can just hold us and speak to us?

We tend to use more words than we have to. The child in the arms of the parent, lovers in an embrace or simply sitting next to each other holding hands don't need words. Sometimes words are an obstacle that separate rather than unite us.

Just to be with the Lord is so beautiful. We know our God dwells within us. We don't make God present by many and beautiful prayers; God is present in us. The prayer of simplicity is a prayer in which by our presence, faith, love, and silence we allow ourselves to be totally present to our God. It is in this kind of prayer that the Lord does great and wonderful things to us.

Like Jesus, we leave the holy place of prayer and we go to minister to our sisters and brothers in his name. When we do that, our ministry is simply sharing the love of God that we have first experienced in prayer.

## The Faith of the Canaanite Woman

MATTHEW 15:21-28

*Wednesday of the Eighteenth Week of the Year*

This is quite a scene. The Canaanite woman is shouting after Jesus, and the disciples can't shut her up. "Lord, son of David, have pity on me! My daughter is terribly troubled by a demon." The disciples plead with Jesus to get rid of her. She's embarrassing them.

It seems there's a two-way healing in this scene. The Canaanite woman, because of her persistence and faith, gets her request. Her daughter is healed. But Jesus also learns something this day that maybe he had forgotten: there's nothing stronger than a mother's love. A mother will not take no for an answer, even if it's the Son of God.

Even with his logical explanation of not throwing bread to the dogs (which was kind of insulting) the woman turns it all around in the most beautiful statement of humility, saying that even the dogs eat the crumbs from the table.

I think Jesus left the scene a little wiser. I think he knew from that day on that you never say no to a mother's prayer. Maybe that's why Mary's prayers have such power. After Cana's wedding feast and the words of the Canaanite woman, Jesus must have promised himself that he'd never say "no" to a mother's prayer again.

Maybe, too, the Canaanite woman taught Jesus a little lesson in manners, especially on how to talk to a woman who is upset about her daughter's spiritual life. Even the Son of God had to grow and stretch. As much as Jesus taught all whom he met and preached to, there were also those who taught him a thing or two. The Canaanite woman was one, his Mother Mary another, and I bet Peter's mother-in-law was a third. No matter who we are, we can learn, especially from the poor and simple.

Are we listening to the wisdom of the little ones around us? We all know the holy ones around us. We should not be embarrassed to ask those whom we know speak to God for their opinion or guidance. God always calls the weak, the simple, and the humble to confound the vain and the poor. There are many Canaanite women around who'd love to give us a piece of their mind. Are we brave enough to ask?

## Peter's Declaration About Jesus

MATTHEW 16:13-23

*Thursday of the Eighteenth Week of the Year*

"Who do you say that I am?" That's a very direct question. Jesus addressed it to Peter and the disciples. He did so after inquiring what others are saying about him. Some say so and so, others say so and so. That's so easy because it really is just repeating gossip. But when Jesus looks us in the eye and says to us: "Who do *you* say I am?" it's a bit different. It is a demanding response and personal commitment. We have no one to hide behind. We express our hearts and our belief.

A lot of Christianity is lived hiding behind other people's faith and their statement of it. The priest, the teacher, the pope—all have their place in our formation. There comes a moment when it's no longer enough to

155

hide in the shadow of someone else's faith. There comes that moment when we have to say: "I believe." I believe because it makes sense to me. It is true. It is real. Jesus Christ is the living Son of God. He is my Savior and Lord and I give my life to him and desire to follow him to the best of my ability.

A child's faith is a beautiful thing for a child. It is inappropriate for an adult. A faith that has been tested and analyzed and worked through is the faith that is worthy of an adult, that will sustain that adult through his or her lifetime.

This adult faith is always in flux. Just as Jesus grew in faith and struggled with doubts and questions and felt abandoned by the Father, so will we. As we pray over Jesus in the Garden of Olives and Jesus on the cross, we see great struggle, agony, and, at times, even doubt. Why is this happening? Where is my Father? What does all this mean? We have all said these words in our prayers, and so did Jesus say and feel them in his prayer.

It is after a Christian has gone through a crucible of life and had to make real decisions for Christ that he or she is able to say: "You are the Christ, the Son of the living God," and mean it and understand it. It is then a Christian has learned the meaning of the faith of an adult and believes in a beautiful and magnificent way.

The faith of a child on first communion day is touching and beautiful. The faith of a man or woman coming to the eucharist for help in a problem and guidance in a struggle is magnificent. That faith is like the faith of Jesus in his struggles and doubts.

# Take Up Your Cross

## MATTHEW 16:24-28

*Friday of the Eighteenth Week of the Year*

In the great trial scene of Sir Thomas More in *A Man for All Seasons*, Sir Thomas looks upon the perjurer Richard Rich wearing the emblem of office and says to him, "Richard, it says in scripture what does it profit a man to gain the whole world and lose his soul—but for Wales!"

It was the same line from scripture that St. Ignatius Loyola repeatedly spoke to Francis Xavier as he tried to catch that big fish, convert him, and make him a Jesuit. Of course, Ignatius succeeded, and the rest is history.

There have been many big fish converted by these words of scripture. These words force us to look at what we are doing with our lives and to ask ourselves if this is what it's all about.

The church does this on Ash Wednesday when it reminds us of our approaching death. The liturgy of a funeral has those elements. The church is not afraid to remind us that we will die and to ask us if we are ready to meet the Lord.

If we live in true discipleship, we are ready. If we take up our cross each day and follow in the footsteps of Jesus then we can say with good Pope John: "My bags are packed!"

All of this is not meant to be maudlin or negative. On the contrary, the most life-giving thing is to know we are living as Christ's disciples. To know that we are at peace with ourselves, our God, and our neighbor produces in us a joy and a zest for life. We are filled with life and hope when we know that we walk with Jesus and follow in his footsteps.

The scriptures challenge us to ask ourselves if we are doing anything to hurt ourselves. Are we walking in harmony and peace with all creation? Are we giving a creature or thing or person the adoration and love that only God deserves? Are we worshipping money, prestige, our own will, or our physical and sexual appetites before the loving God and his Kingdom?

What have we gained if we have everything except God and his Kingdom? Maybe as we look into our hearts from the perspective of this scripture we will feel the need and the desire to make some changes. What a blessing that would be—to allow the word of God to bring us closer to the Lord and his Kingdom. In so doing, the love of God will be our first and greatest pleasure, and nothing will ever take its place, not even Wales.

## Jesus Cures a Boy With a Demon

### MATTHEW 17:14-20

*Saturday of the Eighteenth Week of the Year*

The disciples have a lesson to learn today that is not very pleasant. Jesus is angry with them because their lack of faith prevented them from curing the demented son of a loving father. The father had gone to the disciples for help, but they weren't able to do anything for him. This good father loved his boy so much that he went directly to Jesus and asked him to cure him. Jesus touched the boy and called the demon out of him and the boy was cured.

Afterward, the disciples, crestfallen and disappointed in their own inability to help the boy, ask Jesus why they were unable to do so. Jesus tells them the truth and it hurts. They don't believe enough. Their faith is weak. Jesus continues by telling them what their ministry would be like if they truly believed. They could move mountains. They could do wonderful things for people in God's name.

Sometimes our prayer is like the disciples'. We don't believe enough and that is why nothing happens. Every healing miracle of Jesus is dependent on the faith of the recipients of the grace and of the ministers. If you observe normal Catholic worship and life there is very little "going out on the limb" kind of prayer. It is only in the context of a praying and believing community that signs and wonders occur in any way at all. We seem to pray as if we do not expect anything to happen. We demand little in our prayer and get little. We hide behind the words of the ritual and sacramentary because we are afraid to say: "Father, in the name of your Son, the Lord Jesus Christ, I demand this healing right now!" What usually happens is that we explain away what we are half-heartedly asking in saccharine and meaningless phrases that neutralize the power of our prayer. We are just like the disciples and we deserve Jesus' anger as he says to us: "What an unbelieving and perverse lot you are!"

Thank God that the Lord calls many holy people into the healing ministry. People like Dennis Kelleher, CSSR, have preached to and prayed over tens of thousands of sick and troubled people. They have reminded the church that Jesus heals today just as he did when he walked this earth. He heals now through the hands, faith, and love of people like Dennis Kelleher. Thank God for the charismatic renewal that calls the church to come together and stand on the word of Jesus and demand the graces and healing we so need.

As we open our hearts to the power of the Holy Spirit, we pray for an increase in faith, so that we will all pray together: "Father, in the name of your Son, the Lord Jesus Christ, we demand this healing, right now! Amen!"

# The Temple Tax

MATTHEW 17:22-27

*Monday of the Nineteenth Week of the Year*

A dark shadow falls upon the hopes and dreams of the disciples—the cross. The shadow of the cross darkens and depresses all the hopes the disciples have of glory, power, and success. Jesus, the Messiah, comes not to be king, but to be the suffering servant, he who will lay down his life in loving service to the community. That means that those who follow and serve him must be part of the same mystery of dying to self so that a new and greater life may come forth. The disciples were looking forward to all the wonderful things of the world—fame, money, and power. Jesus dashes their dreams by inviting them and us into the Paschal Mystery.

We who follow Jesus today can sometimes make the mistake that the disciples did. We can create a church that brings us blessings, comfort, consolation, and even financial rewards. If we do that at the expense of ignoring the Paschal Mystery, we no longer are following Christ—just ourselves and our own ambitions.

We who follow Jesus are called to give our lives in loving service to others. No matter what our vocation happens to be, in love is how it must be lived. Love is giving ourselves totally to the one we love. It is giving our life to the little flock that the Lord has given us to care for.

When the church becomes too concerned over worldly power and materialism it is forgetting its call to be the humble servant of the world. When it becomes one in love and service to the poor, it becomes truly powerful and the irresistible presence of Christ in the world.

Jesus and the church and each of us are to be a sign of contradiction. What are we contradicting? We contradict the values of the world. We shout out by the way we live that love, gentleness, mercy, compassion, kindness, and poverty are the most powerful signs in the whole world, and when we live in this seemingly "weak" manner we are truly powerful. Nothing is more powerful than the cross that leads to resurrection.

## Like Little Children

MATTHEW 18:1-5; 10:12-14

*Tuesday of the Nineteenth Week of the Year*

"Who is of the greatest importance in the kingdom of God?" This question of the disciples expresses a real concern on their part about status and pecking order in the Kingdom. It is very important to them who will be on top and who will be beneath them. It is the raw desire for power, status, and success in the hearts of those who should have known better, the ones closest to Jesus.

In many ways, today's gospel continues the theme of yesterday's as Jesus teaches his way of life that is so different from the way of worldly wisdom and knowledge. Jesus points to a child as a symbol of who is great in his Kingdom. The little one, the poor one, the innocent one is the one who is great in God's eyes. Jesus, pointing to the child, tells the disciples that if they want to enter the Kingdom they must become like the child. They must be humble, honest, and transparent.

Jesus then goes on to speak to the disciples and to us about how precious a child is in God's eyes. No one is more important to the Lord than his little ones who must be protected, loved, and cared for like the Christ Child. Every child is the Christ Child given to us to love and cherish.

The church should burn with a passion for the rights of children. We should be in the vanguard of our society fighting for the well-being of all of our children.

The church is pro-life. It defends the right to life of every baby in the womb. It defends the right to a decent life for all of our children who are born into poverty and who lack the basic human needs of nourishment, housing, clothing, and education. What a terrible thing it is for our society and world to see children as the victims of war, abuse, drugs, and violence.

What a blessing and joy it should be for parents when Jesus tells them that as they so lovingly accept, cherish, and care for their children, they are actually doing these beautiful things to Jesus. That is why loving parents have such a special place in the Kingdom of God, and that is why caring for and cherishing our children must be our first priority.

## Confronting Wrong Actions

MATTHEW 18:15-20

*Wednesday of the Nineteenth Week of the Year*

Jesus teaches us today about two very important aspects of community life: mutual correction and common prayer. As always, Jesus is direct, honest, and to the point. He tells us if anyone has anything against a brother or sister, they should go right to that person and tell them what is in their heart. Jesus urges us to face disagreements honestly and squarely.

This is tough talk for church groups and most other groupings of people. The number of people who will honestly share with another what bothers them is very small. We talk around, behind, under, and most of all about people. We do precious little talking *to* them.

It's not easy to confront someone. It's easier to ignore the hurt or talk to other people about the person who has hurt us. When we live in the truth of Jesus we learn to speak in honesty and love to one another. A person who has grown in the spirit of truth learns to say what they mean and mean what they say.

When a brother or sister will not listen to us, Jesus advises us to bring in the church, other Christians, to speak with and for us for the well-being of the friend. What a blessing it is to be part of a family or community that is able to love and challenge in unison.

This is what is operative when friends and family are able to confront a loved one about drinking, drugs, gambling, or other addictions. It is a holy moment when they stand together in love and tell the person that they have a problem. They do it out of love because they are concerned with the well-being of the loved one. The truth spoken in love is irresistible and undeniable—it is one of the strongest forces in the world. Jesus invites us to build communities where the truth is a friend, not an enemy.

Jesus calls us to be that family where truth and honesty flow from a deep faith and prayer life. When our homes and parishes are places like that, they are places of peace, truth, and love.

## Forgiveness

MATTHEW 18:21–19:1

*Thursday of the Nineteenth Week of the Year*

Seventy times seven! How much Jesus expects of us. How can we even begin to measure up to this demand and precept of Jesus?

Forgiveness is so difficult for us. It's almost impossible in human terms and psychology to forgive after repeated serious hurts. How can a son or daughter really ever forgive a parent who didn't love them as they deserved, or who even physically or sexually abused them? How can a spouse ever forgive their mate who abandoned them or was unfaithful to them? The list of deep and profound hurts knows no end. It is impossible to forgive as Jesus calls us to forgive unless Jesus is given the responsibility for doing it.

There are moments in our lives when we just can't do it. All we can do is come to Jesus and say to him, "Lord, I can't forgive what they've done to me or to my family. Please, Jesus, take my hate from me. Take my feelings, Lord. I give it all to you. I want to do what you want me to do. Jesus, you have to do the forgiving—you have to do the loving for me."

This kind of forgiving is what we're capable of doing, the forgiving of Jesus in us. We pray to Christ, the gentle healer, to touch our hearts, to take the old bitterness from us, and to help us to give to others the forgiveness that we have so often begged from Christ.

When we think and pray about our own sins and the things we have done to offend the Lord and how he has so graciously and lovingly forgiven us, we have no choice but to give that same gift of compassion and mercy to others.

Our God's forgiveness knows no limits. We always have another chance. There is always a new beginning. We are never discarded by our God. Don't we have to give the same break to our sisters and brothers who offend us?

"Forgive us our trespasses as we forgive those who trespass against us." Amen.

## Marriage

MATTHEW 19:3-12

*Friday of the Nineteenth Week of the Year*

Today, Jesus speaks to us about marriage. He reminds all of us how precious and sacred this holy sacrament is to the life of the church and to the world.

Many of us have celebrated the funerals of people who are great family people. Funerals like these are very special. First of all, the grief and pain that is experienced by the bereaved spouse when the couple has lived a life of deep love together is most profound. It is shared intensely by their children (and grandchildren too). And yet, in the midst of pain and sorrow, there is a joy and hope because the couple has loved so deeply and completely that there are no regrets and no "If only I had . . ." thoughts or feelings. When a couple is deeply in love and lives that kind of life together, they are most blessed and happy people. They have everything. No matter what life deals them, they can handle it because they have each other. They will celebrate good times and grow closer together in bad times. "I take you as my beloved wife/husband—from this day forward—for better, for worse, for richer, for poorer, in sickness and in health until death do us part." The vows say it all.

The children who grow up in this kind of love and community learn all they have to know for the rest of their lives. They have been given everything. When a husband and wife love each other in this total and Christ-centered love, they cannot help but to love their children exactly as they need to be loved.

Today the church reminds its married couples to remember the gift of love that God has given them in their holy sacrament. The church reminds them never to take their life or their call for granted, but to live it each day. Each day they have to make a decision to love. Each day they are called to love the way Jesus loved, laying down his life in love for his beloved.

The church reminds its married couples of the holiness of their lives. There is still so far to go to truly understand and appreciate the spirituality of marriage. There is still an inferiority complex on the part of some that marriage and child rearing is good and all of that, but it's not really as great or important or holy as priesthood, religious life, or other "churchy" ways of life. How crazy!

When the Lord calls us, he calls us to holiness. Marriage is to be the image of the love between Christ and his spouse, the church. When a man and woman in holy marriage love each other, they love Christ. When they touch each other and caress each other, they do so to Christ. How far we have to go to truly understand that sex in marriage is the most profound expression of love and holiness that can be experienced in this life. It is an experience of God. Sex in marriage is very similar to the intercourse we experience with Christ in receiving holy communion. They are both the most profound and complete expression of communication and love that is possible and available to us.

And yet, neither married sex nor the eucharist can ever achieve this full potential of union and power in our lives unless the totality of our lives is dedicated to loving and unity. Holy communion has no effect on our life unless the whole of our life is the living of a life of faith and prayer in Jesus Christ. Sex in marriage means little unless a couple is loving each other in all the other aspects and activities of life. Sex then celebrates *everything* they are and everything they do.

Our church today thanks you for the love you give to each other, your children, and the rest of the world. The church encourages you never to give up, but to keep on even when it's tough. The church urges you never to settle for an okay or mediocre relationship, but to work for the most passionate, life-giving, and holy relationship possible. And it is *work*! It doesn't just happen! Today the church reminds you that you *are* God's saints as you keep on trying and loving. Make your marriage the most important thing in your life. Put nothing before it, not even your children. Take care of each other—be tender, gentle, forgive each other—never go to sleep angry and without making peace! Go to sleep in each others' arms praying for your children and asking Jesus to bless your home and your love. "Love one another as I have loved you" (John 15:12).

On this World Marriage Day, we are reminded of the call that Jesus gives to our married sisters and brothers to grow in his holiness by loving each other, their children, and the whole body of Christ. The church urges you to do things for yourselves and your marriage. Take the time together you need to deepen, rediscover, or heal your love and your relationship. Give yourself the gift of a Marriage Encounter. If you're having problems, be humble enough to seek counseling or perhaps consider making the Retrouvaille Weekend for troubled marriages. Call your church for more information about both of the weekends. Know that your parish is there to support and help you in your journey together.

Your marriage is so important and precious to the future of the church and the world. Your home and family is the church—the little church where the gospel is experienced in your relationship and the eucharist is constantly celebrated in beautiful simplicity and family life.

## Jesus and the Little Children

MATTHEW 19:13-15

*Saturday of the Nineteenth Week of the Year*

Jesus and the parents and children present a beautiful scene. I present to you "The Trail of the Cheerios" based on this gospel.

### THE TRAIL OF THE CHEERIOS

In preparation for the Sacred Triduum of Holy Thursday, Good Friday, Holy Saturday, and Easter the priests of our parish hear confessions all day long on Wednesday of Holy Week. There are as many as six priests hearing confessions at the heavier times. It is always an exhausting and an exhilarating experience. To share the life of our dear sisters and brothers is humbling and challenging to us. Most of the people who come to the sacrament are so much holier, more generous, and more loving than I could ever hope to be. This sacramental moment is often (to me) an unofficial canonization of God's holy people, God's saints, who are building up the body of Christ by their lives of sacrificial love.

On this particular Wednesday some years ago, the Lord gave me a sign and symbol of the eucharist—his death and resurrection—which was my "peak" moment of Holy Week. One of the penitents who came to confession was a young mother of four. She came into my confession room with a baby under one arm and a collection of bags and other baby accouterments under the other. She was typical of so many holy parents who put Jesus into a very special and real place in their lives. In the midst of all their hard work and struggles the Lord is there, and they do their best to find time to pray and to make all of their unending daily activity the real prayer that it is.

Coming to Mass with four kids under ten is a monumental engineering and organizational project—but come they do. Confession ditto! Come they do! After this particular moving and beautiful confession in which I tried to gently tell her what saints she and her husband truly were (which most people can't comprehend), she left with her squirming and happy baby, apologetic that maybe they had "disturbed" Father. As she left, there was a tear in my eye because I love her and her husband and all the sisters and brothers they represent, and because I see in her the holiness and love of Jesus shining forth in such a powerful and healing way.

After they left I glanced down on the rug and there they were: two Cheerios! Those Cheerios became for me the very essence of what eucharist means and what Holy Thursday and Good Friday symbolize.

For me, the two Cheerios were a new eucharistic bread symbolizing the incredible life of love and devotion of this young wife and mother and all the other spouses and parents she represents. These two Cheerios sacramentalize the dying and the rising that constitute the daily living and loving of God's people.

I picked up the two Cheerios—my special eucharistic bread—and they are on my desk right now reminding me of what priesthood is all about. I pray that I can be the kind of priest that this young mother is. I pray that I can love and give the way she does, day in and day out, when you feel like it and when you don't. I pray that I can live with her passion by loving others first and putting myself second to the family that God has given me to love and serve.

As I look at the two Cheerios I think of Good Friday—the dying to self and pride that this young mother and wife is doing every day. I think of her broken heart when she lost her baby. I think of the financial struggles that never end. I think of the sleepless nights, never going on vacation, never having a day off, not being able to pursue her remarkable talents and career. I think of her faithful and struggling love of her husband. I think of her love for her children for whom she would be willing to die at any moment.

I think of how hard she works to center her family in Christ and to make her home the little church and her table and meals the eucharist. And then I think of the total and uncompromising "yes" she spoke to the Lord and renews to the Lord each and every day.

As I look at the Cheerios I also think of Easter in her life. I see the joy and pride in her eyes as she looks at her husband and her children. I see the profound peace and joy she experiences as she sees her children grow in grace and knowledge. I see what beautiful people her children are becoming because love fills their home and their lives—a love only a mother can give. I see the deepening of the marriage bond that has passed through the beautiful and delightful days of romance and passion to a love tested by self-giving and living for the other. I see the many young women in our community who have been touched by her faith, sisterhood, and friendship.

I look at this beautiful young woman and I see the power of Christ's resurrection shining through her as she epitomizes the worthy wife spoken of in Proverbs, chapter 31.

But most of all I see the resurrection shine forth in her because she is a true saint of Jesus who doesn't have a clue that she is a saint. Her selfless, humble, and loving life is being lived by so many today—in my parish, in our community, and all over the world.

These holy ones are the saints of today. They are the treasure and pride of the church because they are being the church by living out the mystery of Jesus' death and resurrection each day of their lives.

On Holy Thursday, I touched the eucharistic bread of the two Cheerios from the previous day. I realized once again that I am being taught how to be a priest by the example of the saints in my parish—the holy ones who love with all they've got—day in and day out without counting the cost. They are the saints of today and the best part is that they don't even know it.

Of all these saints no one approaches the holiness of single parents who give everything and more to be father or mother. Their whole life is a living out of the life of Jesus the Good Shepherd as they lay down their lives in love for their little flock.

Every day I thank Jesus for the holy ones he has placed in my life to remind me what it means to love and to give one's life in loving service. I thank him for that special eucharistic bread—the two Cheerios—that taught me what eucharist really means. I discovered that Cheerios were left behind in many places that Wednesday. They blessed the floors of supermarkets, drug stores, doctors' offices, friends' dens (where they were gratefully gobbled up by crawling babies and pets).

The eucharist had a long and varied procession in preparation for the procession on Holy Thursday. Every place that was visited by this holy woman became more beautiful and peaceful because love was brought there. It was symbolized by the eucharistic presence of the Cheerios trail. The Lord visited these places because one of his personal friends who has given her life to him and her little flock was there. Where the saints walk, the Kingdom of God is made present. It was very present that Wednesday in Westbury in the trail of the Cheerios.

I thank the Lord this Mothers' Day for the love of my beautiful sisters who hold up for me, by their lives, the image of the loving Jesus who laid down his life for his flock. They do the same. They live out the Paschal Mystery gently but convincingly, inviting me to enter into it with them more and more. By their humble example they call me to nail to the cross my pride, lack of faith, self-concern, pettiness, and selfishness so that I might rise with them and Jesus into the glory and joy of Christ's love.

Family is everything. I also thank the Lord for the gift of my own parents and my dearest sister Rosemary, who is also with God. I am so grateful that in growing up I shared so fully in the eucharist of a mildly crazy and loving family. I am so grateful that I continue to share the eucharist of love and family with my dear sister, Agnes, her husband, Lou, and their beautiful daughters, Laura and Rachel. They love me so much and give me a safe and holy place to call home. Whenever I enter their home I feel the peace and love for Jesus fill every part of my being. I am in a holy place. I am on holy ground. I'm home.

# The Rich Young Man

### MATTHEW 19:16-22

*Monday of the Twentieth Week of the Year*

We all identify with the rich young man. He is such a good fellow and it saddens us as much as it does him that he can't sell all that he has to go and follow Jesus. It saddens us because neither can we go sell all that we have and give it to the poor and completely follow Jesus. We all have things we feel we need and can't live without—whether they're really needs or wants is another question. One thing is for certain, there are very few of us living the evangelical poverty to which Jesus calls his disciples.

We all seem to do all right with living life and keeping the commandments, but perfection, that's another matter. Yes, there are always those special souls like Dorothy Day, Mother Teresa, St. Clare, and St. Francis who totally embrace poverty and make Jesus their total and complete possession. They shine out like diamonds in the crown of the church. They also make the church uncomfortable because they are the living reminder of what Jesus calls us all to be and what we have not yet, and seemingly cannot, attain.

At least they make us a bit less self-righteous and they inspire us to look at what we think we need but really just want. They help us to have a sense of responsibility to those who have little or nothing. They coerce us into sharing and being less possessive and greedy. They do a very important job in calling the church back to the spirit of its Lord, the simple carpenter of Nazareth, who has nowhere to lay his head.

The rich young man is you and I. We will go just so far. Maybe it's really the most and the best we can do. In our sinfulness Jesus still looks upon us with love and he never casts us off. He is always there for us. He will never abandon us. Never!

# The Eye of the Needle

## MATTHEW 19:23-30

*Tuesday of the Twentieth Week of the Year*

"The eye of the needle." It's a symbol that makes us uncomfortable. Most people, when they hear this, kind of breathe a sigh of self-righteousness saying to themselves that this doesn't apply to them, it applies to all those other fat cats who have millions.

Of course, it applies to *all* of us. The key question here is what possesses our hearts? What is the thing that we live for and are willing to die for? What is the thing that rules and motivates our life, our thoughts, and all that we do?

Material possessions can be obstacles for those who have much and for those who have little. Jesus warns those with great possessions that they will enter the Kingdom with difficulty. It is hard to carry and drag all of our possessions to God. They can become an end in themselves.

The person living in the Spirit of Jesus must see every material thing as a blessing and a gift from God. But every material thing has a responsibility that comes with it. When we are blessed, we are expected to *be* a blessing to others by sharing what we have with those who have little or nothing.

Our use of the things of this world is a reflection of how we love and follow Jesus. We know people who are richly blessed but who are also a blessing to so many others. Riches make them more humble, more sensitive, and more concerned about the rights and needs of others. Unfortunately, the opposite also happens, and the eye of the needle becomes a reality in their lives. They can't enter the Kingdom because they're too encumbered.

Where do you and I stand? Are our blessings leading us closer to Jesus? Do we use them as occasions to bless the Lord by sharing them with others? Are we sensitive to the poverty and pain all around us? Do we try to reach out and touch others who need our help?

The eye of the needle is for all of us to ponder. The old image of the power of attachments is good for us to ponder. It goes like this: If a bird is tied with a very thin silk string or a steel cable the result is the same: it can not fly. What is keeping us from flying?

## The Workers in the Vineyard

MATTHEW 20:1-16

*Wednesday of the Twentieth Week of the Year*

This is one gospel I would never want to read at Mass on Labor Day! I could just see the placards and signs describing the employer, who happens to be the Lord, as unfair and crazy.

Yet, that is a pretty accurate description of the Father. He is crazy—crazy in love for us. He is unfair—unfair in giving us what we could never deserve.

The parable of the master and the workers in the vineyard is a very significant one in trying to understand the mercy and love of God. We are so used to justice and fairness as the American way of life, that this gospel ruffles our feathers and challenges us to look at God's justice.

We don't have a problem with a God who is fair or even kind, but when someone turns their back on God all their life and repents at the very moment of death, should they get the same reward as we who have toiled for the Lord in the heat of the day? Isn't that really a slap in the face for those who have worked so hard and been so faithful? Isn't forgiveness like this detrimental to the *esprit de corps* of the good? The gospel simply makes no sense to the way we look at things and do things. There's no justice here.

Of course there's not. The justice and mercy of God are beyond our comprehension and understanding. God's love is a mystery. It is a mystery we cannot comprehend. All we can do is celebrate it and accept it.

No one, even the person who has toiled in the heat of the day, deserves God's mercy and forgiveness. We cannot come near on our own merit to the holiness and purity of God. Our salvation is a pure and holy gift. We can never earn or deserve it. All we can do is accept it like the workers who came in the late afternoon.

We are all those late afternoon workers, and our prayer is that of the good centurion: "Lord, I am not worthy. Say but the word and my soul shall be healed." In our holy faith we worship the God of unending mercy, the one who waits and waits until we finally come home. God does this because God loves us.

## The Parable of the Wedding Banquet

MATTHEW 22:1-14

*Thursday of the Twentieth Week of the Year*

Again Jesus refers to the Kingdom in terms of a banquet, a wedding banquet, which the king gives in honor of his son. The servants go out spreading the wonderful news that a banquet has been set for the king's son. They invite all with invitations of "please come—all is prepared."

The response of the would-be guests is the story of salvation history to our present day. Some simply ignore the invitation. They are so taken up with their business and concerns that they just don't want to be bothered.

Others not only ignore the invitation but become abusive to those who make the announcement. Some even do harm and murder the messengers. How much we see of this in our day. How many messengers have shed their blood and given their lives because they made the announcement of the good news!

The soil of countries like El Salvador has been made red with the blood of Oscar Romero, the Jesuits, and the holy women, not to mention the thousands of nameless compesinos. The story of the invitation is being lived out in each and every community where the gospel of justice and peace is being preached and people are being called to a new and abundant life.

The Lord never gives up. The invitation continues to be given. All are called to sit down at table with the Lord and sup. Everyone belongs. Everyone is a child of this loving God.

The poor and the humble seem to have the wisdom and simplicity to know the treasure of God's love and invitation. Let us not allow any of the loud voices of our society to distract us from accepting the invitation.

## The Greatest Commandment

MATTHEW 22:34-40

*Friday of the Twentieth Week of the Year*

"Teacher, which commandment of the law is the greatest?" The Pharisees ask Jesus one of the most important questions of life, not because they want to learn or grow, but because they want to trick Jesus up and discredit him.

What an example of how learning, knowledge, and position hurt rather than give life and hope! The same thing can happen to us in the church.

Sometimes God becomes a thing or a commodity for us. We can become very glib and free with discussing every aspect of God and the church. We can know all the correct terminology, all of the "in" words and phrases, all of the latest trends and movements, and have absolutely no clue as to who Jesus Christ is and what he means in our daily life.

It is a dangerous thing when theologians, teachers, parents, and preachers talk about God but have little personal and deep knowledge of God. The higher one becomes in the responsibility of teaching and preaching the word, the more one must be living in submission to the movement of the Holy Spirit in their life.

The Pharisees' question to Jesus is wonderful. The answer Jesus gives is the summary of all spiritual and religious searching. He has given them the answer to everything. Yet, can they hear it? Can they receive it? Can they live it?

Are we able to hear the answer? Can we receive it? Can we live it? We have heard the words so many times. We have become so accustomed to them that we have memorized them and can quote them. Have they ever soaked in and really touched our hearts? Are they just too simple and familiar for us to take seriously? Do we believe that the Lord is speaking personally to us right now as if for the very first time?

To hear him means putting aside all preconceived answers. It means coming to him as an open vessel waiting to be filled. It means not having the answers until Jesus gives them. It means standing humbly before the God of surprises not knowing what will be up his sleeve today.

Imagine! Love God with all your heart, all your soul, all your strength. Love your neighbor as yourself. Imagine what would happen if we tried it!

# "Do Not Follow Their Example"

## MATTHEW 23:1-12

*Saturday of the Twentieth Week of the Year*

Many scriptures make me feel uncomfortable. This one makes me squirm. Imagine if the Lord were saying these terrible things about you or me!

Imagine him saying that I sit in the chair of Moses and that my people should listen to what I teach, but that they should *not* imitate my example!

Reading on, the picture gets worse: binding up heavy loads and placing them on people's backs, not lifting a finger to help, doing good things only to be seen and praised. Jesus rails against this kind of false religion. But it's so easy to slip into!

Jesus calls us to be a church of service, a church of humility and gentleness. It's so easy for the priest, parent, teacher, or for anyone in authority to exercise power rather than humbly serve.

I hate this gospel; I see too much of myself in it. I see too much of my own tendency to glorify and serve myself and my own agenda. Religion too easily becomes for me a comfortable lifestyle. It's nice to be the king!

It's great to hear the "Yes, Fathers" and "No, Fathers." It's so easy to think you're important, that you're somebody. When I read this gospel, I see too many descriptions of myself that I don't like. How do you feel when you read this gospel? Thank God we have another chance to change the ending of this story. There *is* hope for us.

Thank God we always have another chance to change the ending of our story. This salvation and life is in store for us if we choose. Jesus gives us such a direct and foolproof path to follow: "The greatest among you will be the one who serves the rest."

# The Scribes and the Pharisees (Part 1)

MATTHEW 23:13-22

*Monday of the Twenty-First Week of the Year*

Today we begin the first of three days on which the gospel begins "Woe to you scribes and Pharisees." These three days are the most negative of all the year. They present Jesus condemning the religious leadership of his time.

On each of these days we find Jesus using the word "fraud" to describe these people. As we read all the things that Jesus rails against, we realize that these words are not just part of an historical event, but they are pertinent to our own lives and ministries today. The scriptures are a two-edged sword. It cuts deep and it calls us to conversion and change of heart and life.

We have to be brutally honest with ourselves. Are the things that Jesus condemns part of our way of life? Do we take the easy way out too often? Is our life and ministry one of adoration, love, and service to the Lord and to his body the church, or is our well-being our main concern? Do we worship the Lord or do we worship ourselves and what we want? There is a very common temptation to use the scriptures to judge others, or to see the scriptures condemning and calling ourselves to account, rather than seeing them as our own personal daily reality check to see if we are walking faithfully with the Lord.

That word "fraud" haunts us. I personally won't mind being described at my Judgment as weak, sinful, human, broken, or unwhole; but fraud, that's another thing. Fraud means that my life is a lie. It means that I say one thing and do another. It means that I teach one thing to others but would never think of trying to live it myself. It means that everything I do is a show and has no sincerity or truth to it. It means that I appear to be loving and caring but really don't care about anybody but myself.

Dear Lord, please don't ever say of me what you said of the scribes and Pharisees. Give me the grace to change.

## The Scribes and the Pharisees (Part 2)

MATTHEW 23:23-26

*Tuesday of the Twenty-First Week of the Year*

As Jesus continues the "woe to you" condemnations, he calls, the scribes and Pharisees blind guides and blind fools. They shut the doors of the Kingdom of God in the faces of the people and do not enter themselves. Our beautiful call, no matter our vocation, is to enter the Kingdom and to take the hand of a sister or brother to lead them in. This is especially true of parents, teachers, and clergy. If we do not open the door and enter, then how can those in our care ever be able to enter? We go to all lengths to make a convert, and that is wonderful; it also puts another demand upon us to cherish and protect the little flock that Jesus has given to us to shepherd and protect. When we give another the gift of faith and life, we have an even greater responsibility to that person to be mentor and guide to what it means to belong to Jesus.

Jesus continues his teaching to us by reminding us what is really sacred—not the gold or the gift in the Temple but God represented by the altar. His next observation and condemnation is to tell the scribes and Pharisees that the external appearance of a person is not what matters but rather what is in the person's heart—the outside of the cup is cleaned but the inside is filled with filth, loot, and lust. Jesus tells us to clear our hearts so that God will be comfortable there.

Jesus condemns the scribes and Pharisees for their injustice. They religiously observe laws on tithing but forget what really matters to God: justice and mercy to the poor. We can't feel justified because we keep some of the law (that which makes us feel good) while neglecting those things that really matter.

Again, we realize that all these "woes" are meant for us to look at our life to see if we really belong to the Kingdom or if we seek our own kingdom. The sword cuts very deep in our hearts.

## The Scribes and the Pharisees (Part 3)

MATTHEW 23:27-32

*Wednesday of the Twenty-First Week of the Year*

It gets hard to read these "woes," to pray about them, and I assure you to write about them. Enough already! And yet, still another day and the whole church must proclaim this gospel and allow it to touch our hearts. So here we go again.

"Woe to you scribes and Pharisees, you frauds! You are like whitewashed tombs, beautiful to look at on the outside but inside is full of filth and dead men's bones." The old translation used the term "whitewashed sepulchers." That says it all, doesn't it?

How terrible it would be to be the fraud, the one who *appears* so clean, beautiful, attractive, holy, and good but in reality is steeped in sin and death.

This is not what the Lord wants of us. He wills our peace and our joy. Jesus is in our lives to rescue us from the things that drag us down. He is there for each of us to be Savior and friend.

If there are areas of our lives that we find uncomfortable, areas that we are helpless and powerless in, we need to use the same beautiful spirituality of AA and admit to the Lord that we are powerless and that we need him. It is the admission that is the beginning of the healing. Once Jesus is with us we are not alone.

Each day our daily prayer allows us to touch him and to be strengthened and nourished by his love and power. As Paul tells us when we are weakest, we are strongest when Jesus is with us. The saint is the sinner who never gives up. Jesus will never let go of us when we call out to him.

The "woes" become "blessed are you" when we give Jesus our brokenness and allow him to live in our hearts. Many of the scribes and Pharisees heard an invitation to which they could not respond. We hear a call from the One who loves us most and who promises always to be there for us. Let us not ignore that call.

## Stay Awake!

MATTHEW 24:42-51

*Thursday of the Twenty-First Week of the Year*

Today the gospel continues the serious tone of the "woe to you" days as Jesus tells us that we must be prepared for the coming of the Lord. He illustrates his point by telling the parable of the return of the master to the household and how the servant must be ready for the master's return at the moment when he is least expected.

The story is a reminder to us that we must be prepared. We do not know the hour at which the Lord will come for us. We do not know when we will die.

While this Gospel may cause concern and worry for some, it is not meant to do so. The Christian is called to live in a very simple and honest way. We are called to live as if each day we live is our last day. We are invited to live in confidence and faith that the Lord will sustain us and strengthen us and that his grace will always be present for us.

The most important thing in our lives is the living of each day in faith and in love. We are not called to do the extraordinary, but the ordinary and the seemingly boring things of everyday life, and to do them with great love.

There is a story of one of the desert fathers. One of his disciples came upon him cooking a meal for a feast day. The young man was shocked to see the abbot so involved in such a worldly pursuit. The young monk asked the abbot: "Father, what would you do if an angel told you that the Lord was returning to earth today?" The abbot didn't miss a beat as he answered: "I'd finish cooking the meal, after all, the Lord may be hungry when he arrives."

So, let's keep on cooking those meals and doing all those good things that Jesus wants us to do to make this world a beautiful place, his Kingdom on this earth. We'll never be afraid of him returning when we're doing his work on earth. When we are we can say what good Pope John said in the face of death: "My bags are packed!"

## The Parable of the Ten Virgins

MATTHEW 25:1-13

*Friday of the Twenty-First Week of the Year*

Today's gospel continues yesterday's theme of being ready for the Lord's coming in the story of five foolish bridesmaids and five wise bridesmaids. The story that is so familiar ends with the Lord saying to the five foolish bridesmaids: "I do not know you."

This is not the easiest gospel. It speaks of preparedness. When the foolish bridesmaids asked the wise ones for some oil, the wise bridesmaids were not being selfish in refusing them some of their oil. There are some things we can only do for ourselves.

No one can give us those basic things that we neglect to give ourselves. No one can read for us, study for us, learn to love for us, or come to know Jesus for us. We have to do these things for ourselves. When Jesus says to the foolish ones: "I do not know you," it is because they have failed or refused to allow the Lord to know them. They have filled their lives with so many things but not with Jesus. They have had time for everything but him.

Living faithfully each day is a process as sure and as gentle as the rain giving life to the parched soil. The Lord comes to us each day as we make time and space for him. He gives life to the soil of our hearts. He encourages us, calls us, affirms us, and gives us hope each day, every day. There is nothing more essential in the life of the believer than giving Jesus the space and time to love us, making an appointment with him, if you will, each day.

No one can do this for us. No one can give us their oil. They can only encourage us to find our own oil. We find the oil, the love of Jesus, each day. Our faith, our work, our love, and our prayers enable us to come to him and know him.

It is this gentle, consistent, and faithful way that leads us to him so that he will be able to say when we knock at the door: "I know you. Enter." When we fail and get sidetracked and forget him, he is always there to lead us back. We can always begin again.

## The Parable of the Talents

MATTHEW 25:14-30

*Saturday of the Twenty-First Week of the Year*

Today's gospel is the parable of the talents. It's one that we frequently hear preached, but I'm not sure that anyone really understands its meaning. Is it about work, productivity, and creativity, or is it simply about being open to grace?

Perhaps the talents are actually the life of Jesus in our hearts. What do we do with that life? Do we allow Jesus to live and grow within us, or do we put him to the side, "buy" him and his grace?

The grace that each of us receives is perfect for us. We all have the potential to be filled with the spirit of his love, but we have to allow that spirit to grow in us. We have to work on it. We have to give it our time and our best. We have to cooperate.

Many people do not live bad lives; they do not throw the grace away, but they never let it become what Christ intended it to be. They bury it. They keep it safe, but they do nothing to allow it to grow. They never come to the potential their life could have achieved had they taken out the talents, used them, and invested them in doing good.

The third servant does give back the talents intact. But we can't just return what we've received. Love is too dynamic and powerful. Its energy demands growth and new life. To bury it and keep it safe misses the whole point of what life is all about.

What Christ gives us is meant to multiply many times over. It is like the bread in the hands of Jesus. It is blessed and broken, and it becomes the food of the multitudes. It is the life-giving presence of Jesus that we are custodians of. His life must be shared with the world. The more we give away the more we have.

*The*
*Gospel*
*According*
*to*
*Luke*

# The Rejection of Jesus at Nazareth

*Monday of the Twenty-Second Week of the Year*

We begin to read today from the Gospel of Luke. In the preceding twenty-one weeks we have read from Mark and Matthew's gospels. In the next thirteen weeks we will read from the Gospel of Luke. In reading from Matthew, Mark, and Luke here, we are not presented with the infancy, early life, or passion accounts. They are reserved for their proper seasons. During the great fifty days of Easter we read from John's gospel.

This is ordinary time, if anyone could ever call anything about Jesus, incarnation, and redemption "ordinary"! This time presents the daily bread of the word to nourish us and sustain us in our day in and day out living and loving. It is the answer to our request to the Lord to give us our daily bread so that we won't faint on our way.

Today's gospel speaks of that very exciting moment in Jesus' life when he returned to his hometown of Nazareth and went to the synagogue. All of Jesus' family and friends were there and no doubt very proud of "their" Jesus who was making a name for himself.

The Book of Isaiah, the prophet, was handed to Jesus to read. He unrolled the scroll and read from Isaiah. "The Spirit of the Lord is upon me; therefore he has anointed me. . . ." When Jesus rolled up the scroll, he handed it to the assistant and began his sermon. He told the people, some of whom knew him from childhood, that he was the fulfillment of all that Israel had hoped and dreamed for. He was the fulfillment of Israel's prophecy.

Initially the audience was enthralled with what Jesus had to say, and then there was a change of mood that led the townsfolk to expel Jesus from the synagogue and the town.

Jesus was challenging them for their lack of faith, but they couldn't take him seriously because they were so familiar with him.

Sometimes we become so familiar with the word of God that we don't allow it to reach and touch our hearts. Let us not drive out Jesus from our synagogue, our town, because we don't take what he says seriously. Don't let familiarity breed contempt.

## The Cure of a Demoniac

LUKE 4:31-37

*Tuesday of the Twenty-Second Week of the Year*

Jesus commands the demon to leave the man in the synagogue at Capernaum. The demon has just shrieked out, ordering Jesus to leave it alone. The demon also does something that many around Jesus could not or would not do: it identifies Jesus as the Holy One of God. As often happens, evil recognizes love and holiness while "the good" are too preoccupied with their piety to truly acknowledge God in their midst.

Jesus commands the demon: "Be quiet! Come out of him." We all stand before the Lord with our own personal "demons," our brokenness, our sinfulness. The voices of these demons are loud and persuasive. They remind us of our broken promises, our guilt, and our sin. They assure us that God can't really love us because we have been too unfaithful. We are not worthy of God's love. We are doomed to exist in a state of bland mediocrity, not evil enough to deserve hell, but certainly not good enough to merit real forgiveness, real love, and real relationship with Jesus.

The strident voices do their best to drown out the constant and faithful voice of Jesus that is always calling us home to him.

Can we see and believe that this story is our story? Can we believe that we are the man in the synagogue of Capernaum? Can we believe that Jesus loves us in the same way that he loves this man, and that he has come into this world to bring us the same freedom and the same liberation that he gave to this man?

Why can't we find the time and the place to be quiet with him? Why can't we allow him to love us? Why can't we quiet our hearts so that Jesus can command the demons in our lives: "Be quiet! Come out of him!"

As Jesus casts out the demons that oppress us, we may indeed be thrown to the ground. A new life and a new day are sometimes very traumatic and difficult, but he is there with us and for us. Like the man in the synagogue, we will not be hurt as the demons leave us. We will fall into the loving arms of Jesus. He will always protect us and take care of us.

## Jesus Heals Many

LUKE 4:38-44

*Wednesday of the Twenty-Second Week of the Year*

Jesus is the Healer who changes the lives and hearts of all who touch him. Love flows from Jesus as the sick, broken, unloved, and sinful each experience the healing touch that they so need. Jesus continues today to touch the poor, broken, sick, and sinful through his body, the church.

This gospel tells the story of Jesus visiting the home of Simon Peter and healing Peter's mother-in-law. All jokes aside about Peter being angry with Jesus for curing his mother-in-law, I think it reveals something important about Jesus' own needs.

Jesus needed support, affirmation, and love. He needed to be healed from his own loneliness, discouragement, feelings of being misunderstood, fears, and temptations. To read the gospel is to see Jesus as truly human and needing the human healing and touch that only family and friends can give.

I can just imagine Jesus in the home of Peter and his wife. The home was probably filled with kids who loved to be in the arms of Jesus and wouldn't give him a minute's peace. If Jesus loved Peter, how much he must have loved Peter's dear wife and her mother and all those wonderful kids!

When we see Jesus with people in the gospels, we tend to think of how much they needed him. Maybe there were times, like in today's reading, when Jesus needed them much more than they needed Him. Maybe Jesus needed the friendship of a normal family who welcomed him. Maybe Jesus needed the quiet moments with Lazarus, Martha, and Mary more than we could ever imagine. Maybe the reason Jesus was able to leave Peter's home and give himself so completely to the sick and the broken was that he had first been loved and healed himself and had something to give.

Like Jesus, we can never be who and what we are meant to be without the loving support of family and friends. The most important part of our spiritual and ministerial lives is our own experience of love. When we have been loved the way we need and deserve to be, then look out world, we can do anything!

# Jesus Calls the First Disciples

### LUKE 5:1-11

*Thursday of the Twenty-Second Week of the Year*

I don't know if Peter called his boat "Basilica," but there is Jesus sitting in the presidential chair adrift from the shore teaching and preaching. What a beautiful sight, early evening at sunset with families lining the shore listening to what Jesus has to say. What was so remarkable about the teaching of Jesus? Of course, the message was sublime. But it is more than the message. It is he who speaks. Jesus loves these people. He loves them with the love the Father has for him. He loves them with every part of his being. His people know that he loves them. That is what touches them and that is what changes their hearts.

As we try to imitate Jesus as parents, teachers, priests, etc., we realize that the most important and indispensable quality of our relationships, work, and ministries is the love that we bring. There are many things we can fake—love is not one of them. When we communicate love to people, they have no choice but to listen because it is Jesus who is speaking.

Jesus then has Peter go out into the deeper waters, and he orders him to lower the nets. They almost break at the number of fish filling them. The full nets are a powerful image of what the church will be. The nets of Jesus will be filled with so many different and beautiful people. All sizes, shapes, colors, dispositions, and personalities will fill the nets of the church. His church will be the home for all. No one will be excluded. We all belong in that marvelous net.

After this great sign, Jesus tells Peter, James, John, and their shipmates not to be afraid. They will be fishers of men and women. The story ends with their return to the shore and the Gospel says: "With that they brought their boats to land, left everything, and became his followers."

This wonderful story of the call of these men is also our story. Each of us is called by name and appointed to seek out our sisters and brothers to bring them into the great net of his love. The more we realize how much he loves us, the better we become at loving our friends into his arms.

## The Question About Fasting

LUKE 5:33-39

*Friday of the Twenty-Second Week of the Year*

"Yours eat and drink freely!" the scribes and Pharisees tell Jesus. What an understatement! The disciples of Jesus had no clue about organized religious life. They were not at all into fasting, penance, long prayers, or any of the other things that traditionally became part of organized religious practice.

If we just look at the preferred means of ministry of Jesus, it was table ministry. Jesus accepted invitations from anybody, and he made the occasion of meals and fellowship the vehicle for himself to touch people's hearts and bring them into the great net. The disciples were always along for the ride and a free meal and had a great time. Would they have run out of wine at Cana if the boys had stayed home?

It is fascinating to observe that what the followers of Jesus will deny and flee from, Jesus embraces and enjoys. Jesus appears to be in love with life and with people. Jesus doesn't turn his back on or give up anything but sin. Jesus is very worldly and very materialistic in the best sense of those words. He sees the hand of his Father in everything, and thus we hear in the background the words of the Father, as he sees that all he creates in Genesis is good and that men and women are very good.

As disciples follow Jesus in order to save the world and people, they must first love the world and people. While it is true that in the life of a disciple there will be days of fasting, penance, and persecution, the outlook of the disciple is always to give glory and praise to God through the beauty of God's handiwork, creation. St. Francis and St. Ignatius of Loyola were given the great gift of seeing God in all things and leading the church to find and worship the Lord in his creation.

Let us be careful so as not to enter into an escapist spirituality. Let us not see God's creation and world as the enemy but as a gift. While it is true that God's world can be abused and used improperly and even sinfully, that doesn't take away from the fact that creation is our first Bible. We find there the marvelous manifestation of the love and the goodness of God. To see God in all things and in all people is truly to be holy.

## The Sabbath

LUKE 6:1-5

*Saturday of the Twenty-Second Week of the Year*

Jesus continues to clash with the Pharisees. Today, they find fault with the disciples for taking the kernels off heads of corn to eat. They are doing a "work" that is forbidden on the sabbath. This conflict grows more bitter and pointed as the weeks pass by.

The key to the conflict is that the Pharisees see the keeping of the law as their prime responsibility in order to worship and serve Yahweh. This is his Law. This is what he demands of his People because of the Covenant. He is their God and they are his People. To be holy they must obey every part of the Law and its interpretation.

195

Jesus takes a new approach that leads to his death. He places himself above the law and teaches that the purpose of the law includes the well-being of people. "The sabbath was made for man and not man for the sabbath." Perhaps the most telling and daring of all the signs of the new Kingdom is that Jesus not only talks to and associates with sinners, he even eats with them. No good and holy Jew could or would do that because to break bread together meant intimacy and friendship.

We are the beneficiaries of this new approach. Jesus not only seeks us out, but he sits down with us at the table of the eucharist. Unworthy as we all are, we are his honored guests as we take our place next to Him and sup with Him at the great feast of the Kingdom.

With gratitude and joy we pray before holy communion: "O Lord, I am not worthy to receive you, but only say the word and I shall be healed." The eucharist is the most democratic of all meals. You'll find everyone there—saints and sinners, all together, all unworthy but all invited by Jesus to sit down with him and share his meal of love.

As we rise from that table, we go out to meet and invite the other poor hungry beggars just like ourselves. The Christian is the hungry beggar who has found the Living Bread and the joy of his or her life is to share that Bread with all sisters and brothers. Let us not forget how it feels to be hungry. Let us not forget the hunger that is all around us. Let us bring home to the great feast all whom we meet.

# Healing on the Sabbath

## LUKE 6:6-11

*Monday of the Twenty-Third Week of the Year*

The scribes and the Pharisees are watching Jesus and the man with the withered hand like hawks, not because they were hoping to see some deed of love and compassion, but because they were looking for some crime to charge against Jesus. They have eyes, but they were blind to the miracle that was before them that had the power to change them forever.

Sometimes we are just like these blind fools. The Lord has set before us every blessing and grace, and sometimes we just can't see it or appreciate it. One of the great qualities of holy people is that they are aware of what is going on around them. They see the hand of God, and they are grateful for all the gifts of a loving God.

Prayer makes us aware. Prayer opens our eyes to see the glory of God's creation. The saint, the poet, the author, and the musician become aware of the divine presence in all things. No one is more aware than the man or woman whose heart is totally open to God in prayer. In the precious moments when we are in the holy presence, we see the human and the created clearer than anyone else because we also see the divine. When the God of love fills our being, we become more aware and more sensitive to all things, especially the hurts, yearnings, and needs of our sisters and brothers.

Prayer and contemplation bring us closer to our God. This journey to God also brings us closer to one another. Just as the spokes of a wheel move toward the center, they also move closer to each other and become one with the center. The same is true of the spiritual life. We do not become aloof, distant, and cool to people because we know the Lord. The opposite is true: to be filled with a love of God draws us closer and closer to the pain and need of all creation, especially our suffering brothers and sisters.

Thomas Merton is an excellent example of this growth. After years of isolation and prayer in a Trappist monastery, he became more and more filled with a love for humanity and he felt a compulsion to speak out against war, injustice, and poverty.

Our poor scribes and Pharisees couldn't see any of this. Life was in reach for them, but they were too distracted by what could not bring them life. They were so concerned about their position and status that they never really saw or heard anything that Jesus did. Let's turn our hearts to the Lord and look at and listen to what he is saying to us.

## The Twelve Apostles

LUKE 6:12-19

*Tuesday of the Twenty-Third Week of the Year*

Jesus spends the night in prayer in preparation for calling the apostles. Jesus comes to this great decision only after he has been in communion with his beloved Father. The life of Jesus is one in which he constantly seeks communion with the Father. Going up the "mountain" is a regular and essential part of the life and ministry of Jesus. He knows the Father's will because he is in constant union with him.

This example of the prayer life of Jesus inspires us and calls us to the same kind of intimacy and union with the Lord. There are so many definitions of prayer in scripture. Jesus invites us to the prayer of petition in which we ask the Lord for all we want and need. Jesus teaches us how to pray when he teaches us the Lord's Prayer and invites us to the unity of peace and love with the Father. Then there is the simple prayer of heart in which we simply speak and listen to the One who loves us the most. We are like little children in the arms of a beloved Parent who always loves and protects us and always cares for our needs.

In that holy prayer we open up to God all that is in our heart and all that is on our mind. In that prayer we ask God what to do and how to proceed just as Jesus asks the Father about whom he should call to be apostles. All of the important decisions of our lives should flow from our deep and loving dialogue with our God.

If we have a "real" life that never crosses over into our prayer life, we really then are not praying. Prayer should connect with and be a part of our real life. Our relationships, careers, projects, dreams, and work should flow from our walk in faith with God. They should be the fruit of that work, and they should lead us to deeper and more fruitful prayer.

Ultimately, we are called to the beautiful prayer of simplicity where our joy is simply to be in the loving presence of our God and where words are no longer necessary.

May the example of Jesus in prayer lead us to a deeper and more beautiful union with God. May our lives flow from the depth and beauty of that relationship.

## The Beatitudes

LUKE 6:20-26

*Wednesday of the Twenty-Third Week of the Year*

Today we are blessed to hear the very core of the teaching of Jesus as the church proclaims the Beatitudes. The Beatitudes summarize the heart of all that Jesus said and did. The version in St. Luke's gospel is older, more primitive, and more to the mind of Christ. St. Matthew softens them. He says: "Blessed are the poor in *spirit*." St. Luke has no qualifiers! It is: "Blessed are the poor."

In St. Luke's version we see a wide-reaching invitation to the poor and the lowly to come into the Kingdom. This is the place they belong. Their very poverty gives them entrance to the Kingdom and the right to sit at the banquet with Jesus. This gospel has such a great appeal to people who are oppressed and cast aside by society. It is a clear and powerful call to those who have nothing that now they have everything because the Kingdom of God is primarily meant for them.

The flowering of liberation theology in Central and South America flows from this new awareness of God's preferential call to the poor and the dignity of those who have nothing but faith and love. Some of the greatest moments of the church's life occur when the church began to truly believe these words and to reach out in special love to the poor. The names of Camara, Romero, and Day become a litany of the modern saints whose names are written forever in the hearts of the poor.

As we pray over the Beatitudes of Luke, they force us to look at and reflect upon what we have done with the gifts and blessings the Lord has bestowed upon us. We have no choice but to look at our own lifestyles to see if they reflect the love and poverty of Jesus, the poor One who comes to bring life and love to all people, but especially the poor.

## Love for Enemies

LUKE 6:27-38

*Thursday of the Twenty-Third Week of the Year*

In today's gospel Jesus takes us to a place that confuses and frightens us. He takes us into the very heart of God as he calls us to be like God and to live in perfect love with ourselves, God, and all of creation. This gospel is the greatest challenge we will ever come upon in the scripture. It can also be the most discouraging because we are not capable of living it on our own. It is beyond human ability and strength. It is a call to be like God and to live in perfect charity and forgiveness to all people.

We can only begin to walk in this path through the power of the Holy Spirit. It is the Spirit who teaches us how to love, who takes our hand and leads us to the Father. This life of love presumes the deepest possible life of faith and hope. It supposes that we have given the Lord the gift, of our love and that we hold back nothing from him.

We pray that God will continue to call us to this sublime life of love. We cannot live it or do it on our own. It is a gift, and we must humbly beg of God the gift of desiring to love as God has loved us.

This is the ethic and the true morality of Jesus. It is not legalistic and institutional. It is communitarian. It is a life lived in the family of faith and service to all.

Let us pray for the gift of desiring this great love. Let us pray for the courage to follow Jesus. Let us ask for the grace of laying down our lives in love for the family of Christ, his holy body, the church.

To grow in holiness is to grow in the mystery of this love. It is to allow Jesus to possess and be a part of every fiber of our being. It is the best way possible to become another Christ, the Love of all.

## Do Not Judge

LUKE 6:39-42

*Friday of the Twenty-Third Week of the Year*

"Hypocrite, remove the plank from your own eye first; then you will see clearly enough to remove the speck from your brother's eye." Jesus calls us who would act as examples or preach to others to first hear and believe ourselves. Christian leadership is primarily a process of modeling those virtues and qualities that we would like to see in another person. It means being the role model for the lesson that we are teaching.

In home life or in parish life, when we are not personally living and treating people with fairness, charity, and justice, then all that we try to teach and witness, whether to our own children or to colleagues, is lost and meaningless. Every project of our life is ultimately about truth, justice, and fairness. Whether it is a question of the institutional church or our own personal relationships, what we are speaks so loudly that nobody can hear what we are saying.

Another way of saying this is that we cannot give what we ourselves do not personally possess. We cannot give virtue, good example, or inspiration to another if we are not already living these things ourselves.

The only real teacher is the person who is personally in the process of conversion. We must be actually working or acquiring those things that we are trying to teach to another. When a child grows up in a home where parents are really trying to love and give their lives for their children and truly trying to live the gospel, then it becomes very easy for their children to "catch" the Christian life from parents who are themselves trying to live it. When people try before anything else to be Christian, the power of Christ's love and presence fills that community.

Let us not be blind guides, but guides who see and know the Lord and follow him. Let us not lead another into the ditch because of our own blindness, but hand in hand let us lead them and ourselves to safety by opening our eyes to the beauty and goodness of God's call.

# A Strong Foundation

LUKE 6:43-49

*Saturday of the Twenty-Third Week of the Year*

" A good tree does not produce decayed fruit any more than a decayed tree produces good fruit."

In today's gospel Jesus speaks of very basic principles of the spiritual life. Good comes from good and evil comes from evil. This principle means that if we want our words and deeds—our fruits—to be good, they must come from hearts that are pure and good.

We simply cannot do the deeds of God unless we first possess the hearts of God. Our journey must be a lifelong process in which we are trying to achieve and develop the loving heart of Jesus.

When we try to be filled with wisdom, goodness, and love of Jesus, we are like those people who build their house upon solid rock. It endures forever because the foundation is rock. When we do not put into our lives the words and heart of Jesus, we are like people who build their homes on sand. When the floods come, they wash away the home and everything else because they have no foundation.

The spiritual life is putting into practice the words of Jesus one day at a time, day in and day out. As that is done, our hearts grow in love and peace with Jesus. Our works and fruits are good and healthy because they flow from Jesus. Our life is built upon the great foundation—the Lord Jesus.

This building doesn't happen overnight. It is the journey of a lifetime. What matters is not that we have reached the destination, but that we are faithful on the journey. Each day he teaches us something more and gives us another gift to make the going easier.

Jesus gently but surely guides us. He won't let us stumble or get lost. His gentle hand will guide us when we wander off course. He will always be there for us to make sure that we reach the destination—eternal life.

## The Faith of the Centurion
LUKE 7:1-10

*Monday of the Twenty-Fourth Week of the Year*

"I am not worthy to have you enter my house." The centurion is one of those blessed people who are filled with the radiance of God's presence and love. The centurion is a man of great position and power, yet is the humble one who acts more like a servant than a master. His sensitivity extends to asking Jesus *not* to come into his house. He says he is unworthy, but he also knows that Jesus would become ritually unclean entering the house of a Gentile.

Isn't it an incredible gift of grace and love the way God touches the hearts of people? This man, a Gentile, was receptive and open to God's touch and power and yielded to the call and grace that God offered him. He was a good man. He walked with God. Jesus says of him that he has not met faith as great as his in all of Israel.

There is something so beautiful and attractive about people who are filled with God's love. Love just flows from them. We delight to be in their presence because we know that the Lord is present. They speak only good about others, they forgive great hurts, and they have the ability to let go of the past with its pain and disappointments and look only to the present with its possibilities and promise.

These holy, humble, and wholesome people don't always fit in the structure of the world because the world does not understand what makes them click. What makes them click is love.

Recently, our parish family prepared for the funeral of one of these "centurions." His name was John Falls, husband, father of seven daughters, grandfather of eight, and deacon of the parish. Jack was one of those beautiful, loving souls filled with the love and joy of Jesus. His whole life was summarized by love, the love of his family and parish. Jack was one of those rare and beautiful souls who could only be described by and defined by love. Dear Jack, pray for us that we allow Jesus to fill us with pure and holy love as you did. Amen! Alleluia!

## Jesus Raises a Widow's Son

### LUKE 7:11-17

*Tuesday of the Twenty-Fourth Week of the Year*

Jesus said to the widow of Naim, "Do not cry," and to the dead young man, "Young man, I bid you get up."

When we see Jesus in this tender moment, I think there are many things going on in him. It is obvious that he pours his heart out to this poor widow who lost her son. But why? Why was Jesus so touched? He had obviously come upon many other tragic scenes like this where people mourned for a loved one. He was not always willing or able to grant such a blessing to others. Why this one?

Perhaps Jesus saw his own mother in the place of the widow. Maybe in his mind's eye he could see Mary weeping over her son Jesus on the day of his burial. Perhaps the image of the Pieta was before his eyes as he identified the suffering and tears of his own mother with this other mother.

What he would not be able to do for Mary he did for the widow of Naim. In this beautiful gesture of love, he has in some way lifted the pain from his own Mother's heart.

Don't we all act so much more charitably when we personally identify with the pain and suffering of others? Don't we reach out in a whole other way when we see ourselves and our loved ones in our suffering, broken sisters and brothers?

The most important reason for the crosses and the pain that we personally experience in life is to make us more sensitive and human to the pain and suffering of others. Henri Nouwen's beautiful image of the wounded healer is a powerful model for everyone's ministry of becoming a truly *human* being.

The heart of Jesus has to be filled with so many emotions this day. As he sees the love of this mother for her boy, he feels the love and tenderness of his mother for him. Maybe Jesus is dealing with guilt because he has had to leave Mary, and was not able to provide for her as he would have liked to. Maybe he is not satisfied with his answers when she asks: "When are you coming home?" and "When are you going to settle down?" Maybe all Jesus can do for his mother is to give the widow of Naim her son back.

## Pleasing God

LUKE 7:31-35

*Wednesday of the Twenty-Fourth Week of the Year*

"The Son of Man came and he both ate and drank, and you say, 'Here is a glutton and a drunkard, a friend of tax collectors and sinners.'"

A bishop friend of mine would say to this scripture: "You're damned if you do and you're damned if you don't!" It's not easy to please everybody. But how we like to! Who likes conflicts and fights—only crazy people!

But there is no avoiding it. If you want to be a person of integrity and principle, you must displease and annoy many people. The only two people we really have to answer to are Jesus and ourselves.

The faith journey of the Christian is supposed to be a journey in truth and integrity. Prayer is so important in this journey as we lay our hearts open to the Lord and seek his counsel and direction. We may not go out looking for it, but we will come upon very important moments when we must make a choice to stand with the Lord or with what is wrong. To stand with Jesus will take a lot out of us, but to stand by evil will destroy us.

We have to make our "best" choices each day. That's all we can do and that's all we should do. Some will hate our choices; others will love them. What matters is: How do we feel about them? Are they our best and most important responses to the Lord's call?

If done in prayer and faith, whatever we decide and choose will be the best choice we can make. If the Holy Spirit has been our guide, then what we come to is the Lord's way for us.

## Jesus Is Anointed by a Sinful Woman

LUKE 7:36-50

*Thursday of the Twenty-Fourth Week of the Year*

What an incredible dinner party this turned out to be! Jesus is at table in the house of Simon, the Pharisee. The guests at the table are all pillars of the community and all greatly respected.

And then this woman, a sinner, crashes the party. She is not interested in the cuisine, drink, or conversation. She is only interested in Jesus. She doesn't speak to him or try to draw him into conversation. She is there to celebrate a liturgy, a liturgy of reconciliation, love, and new beginnings. Even Jesus doesn't know what he's in for! He is going to receive a gesture of love more powerful than any he had ever seen or experienced in his life. This woman will love him in such a deep and profound way, perhaps more intimate than any act of love ever shown to him before. He had done a lot of loving and healing himself. Now he was going to receive a taste of what he had been so generous in giving to others.

The woman opens the bottle of precious ointment and pours it over the feet of Jesus after she has washed them with her tears and dried them with her hair. The aroma and fragrance of that perfume fills the whole house. It has continued to fill the house of the church ever since with its fragrance and purity. That perfume symbolizes pure and total love. This woman obviously recognizes in Jesus the living love of God among people. What she does is respond to the best of her ability to the forgiveness and love that Jesus has given to her. Her love is unconditional, extravagant, and even approaches the bizarre. She loves the way God loves. She holds nothing back, for nothing can be denied the Beloved.

The crowd thinks that Jesus and this woman are both crazy. They are uncomfortable with her love because they are unable to respond to Jesus or love him that way even if they wanted to. They are afraid of what is going on in front of their eyes, and so they try to reduce it to absurdity by talking about the "kind of woman" that touches Jesus. They divert the action of the sacrament with legality and nonsense.

Jesus tries to explain it to them. It all comes down to love. This woman has forgiveness, new life, joy, and peace because she is not afraid to love. The fragrance of the ointment begins to fill our house when we are not afraid to love.

## The Women Accompany Jesus

### LUKE 8:1-3

*Friday of the Twenty-Fourth Week of the Year*

"The twelve accompanied Jesus as he journeyed through towns and villages . . . and also some women." It seems that the band of disciples that accompanied Jesus was definitely co-ed. Not only were the women there, the gospel tells us that they paid for the excursions and supported the ministry.

Leonardo da Vinci's Last Supper has cast an impression of Jesus being surrounded only by men. A recent interpretation of the Last Supper depicts it as more of a family festival with women, children, pets, and the gentlemen surrounding and supping with Jesus. It sounds much more plausible, doesn't it? Would those lovely spouses of the apostles put up with not eating the Passover with their husbands? I don't think so.

Women were such an integral part of the ministry and the life of Jesus. Today as we try to restore women to their rightful place in the church and give them the basic human rights that have been denied them, we would do well to realize that what we are doing now Jesus did when he gathered together his disciples, confidants, and co-workers.

As ministries flourish in the church today, women are bringing their precious gifts to the body of Christ. How blessed are those communities where women exert real leadership and where women and men work side by side as co-ministers of the gospel of Christ.

In God's loving time and providence, we open our hearts to where the Holy Spirit will lead the church in the question of the ordination of women. As we look back on the ancient community, it's not so clear from history that they were not ordained and that what is being sought today is actually only a restoration of what once was.

Let each of us hear and listen to the call of Jesus and respond right now to the best of our ability as we say our "yes" to the Lord. Let's not give up because it's not a perfect church but rather work to bring about his Kingdom in our own hearts and in the hearts of all.

# The Parable of the Sower

### LUKE 8:4-15

*Saturday of the Twenty-Fourth Week of the Year*

Today, Jesus tells us that parable of the farmer going out to sow some seed. Usually, when I think about the parable, I think in terms of Jesus sowing the seeds of faith and the success of the enterprise depending on the disposition of our hearts. The seed will take life only in the heart (soil) ready to receive it. There is always hope. Even when the seed falls on unreceptive soil, the Lord will go out again another day hoping that that will be the day for the seed to fall upon soil where it can take root and grow.

It dawned on me recently that when the seed finally takes root in our hearts and when we embrace Jesus as Lord and Savior, then it is our turn to go out as the sowers of the seed of faith, life, and love. We are all sowers of the seed. We all have the privilege and responsibility of giving back to God's people what God has first given to us.

In our own special vocations and lifestyles we have the opportunity to sow that gift of life and love. Parents do it so effectively to their children as they sow the seed of faith and love in their own families. Teachers, youth ministers, religious workers in business and industry, students . . . we all have the opportunity and possibility of spreading the love of Spirit and sowing that seed. We have such a potential for touching the lives and future of so many people, but like Jesus we have to go out each day and do our job of sowing the seed.

Imagine if Jesus tried to sow that seed in your heart and you weren't ready to receive it. Suppose he gave up and didn't come back the next day or the one after that. Where would you be now if Jesus had given up on you?

That's the great inspiration we have: to be faithful to our call to sow the seed. We have to keep on "keeping on!" We have to keep preaching, teaching, witnessing, and living the gospel.

When the sacred day comes that our friends, family, and associates are ready to receive the word, we will be there and it will be sown and take root. And this new baby crop will in turn begin the sowing, and we will smile and say: "Thank you, Jesus!"

## A Lamp on a Stand

LUKE 8:16-18

*Monday of the Twenty-Fifth Week of the Year*

"No one lights a lamp and puts it under a bushel basket or under a bed; they put it on a lampstand so that whoever comes in can see it."

Why are we so afraid to let our light shine before others? Why are we always hiding behind our faith and our goodness? The theologian Karl Rahner coined the phrase "anonymous Christian." By it he referred to people who were not formally Christian, yet somehow the grace of Christ had touched them and without knowing how or why they were truly Christians.

We are sometimes anonymous Christians in the sense that we do everything we can to hide and cover up our Christianity and faith. For many people, they just don't want anyone to know who and what they are. They are concerned with what is accepted and popular in the secular world. They would never talk about, let alone share, their faith in Jesus Christ.

Perhaps it would really help our faith if we were not ashamed to say to people why we will or won't do something. Maybe it would come a lot easier to walk with Jesus if we weren't afraid to let the world know that we love him and that he's a very important part of our lives.

So many anonymous Christians have bought into this thing of ultimate privacy, that no one should or will know anything about us, especially what is the meaning of our lives.

When we let our light shine just a little bit, we do so much for other people. What a blessing it is when other parents know they are not alone in trying to set standards and values in their homes. What a grace it is for young people to know that there are other kids struggling to do the right thing!

"Let your light shine before all." Don't be afraid or ashamed of Jesus. Profess him and he will help you even more in your walk with him. Lord, Jesus, may the light of your love shine through us that we may bring hope to our sisters and brothers. May we all know that we don't walk alone and that Jesus, our Light, leads the way.

## Jesus and His Family

LUKE 8:19-21

*Tuesday of the Twenty-Fifth Week of the Year*

"My mother and brothers are those who hear the word of God and act upon it." It's hard to believe what Jesus is saying: membership in the Kingdom of God means more than even the flesh and blood relationship of the Mother and Son, Mary and Jesus.

When we ponder this gospel, we begin to see the dignity we possess by being baptized and being part of the family of God. Through the years, preachers and scholars have tried to soften this passage to make it sound like it's really not a "put down" of Mary. It's not a "put down" as such, but it is definitely a realistic statement of the truth: membership and being part of Christ by grace means even more than the physical relationship of being mother and son, even when the son is the Son of God!

Jesus is teaching us the absolute grandeur, beauty, power, and holiness of being part of the family, the church. I don't know if Mary was annoyed with Jesus, but I'm sure that he heard a few good lectures about how he should talk about, and to, his mother. I'm sure she didn't let him off the hook too easily over this one. And yet, what he says is the truth. There is a new order of grace, and everyone can belong to it and be part of it. All we have to do is accept it and enter into it. And, yes, when we do, we become like a mother, brother, and sister to Jesus—we become part of a new creation.

## The Mission of the Twelve

LUKE 9:1-6

*Wednesday of the Twenty-Fifth Week of the Year*

"Take nothing for the journey." In today's gospel, Jesus is giving his plan for pastoral success. We must depend on God, not on money and possessions. So much of what Jesus teaches us in this area can be reduced to putting first things first and not being deceived in giving things power and importance they don't deserve.

It's always fascinating to see how the saints treated money and possessions. The joke is that as St. Francis was throwing his father's possessions out the window embracing Lady Poverty, Don Bosco was outside catching them to give to his boys who lived in the schools and homes he founded for them. Mother Teresa, our modern icon of the little poor one of Jesus, was quite demanding in what she wanted for her poor. She was able to charm a snake to get what she felt the poor deserved. Dorothy Day, who embraced voluntary poverty and lived in the dilapidated houses of hospitality of the Catholic Worker, delighted in listening to classical music on the New York radio stations and the opera from the Metropolitan on Saturday afternoons.

Jesus himself, although he lived simply and poorly, did not live in the abject poverty of the people he preached to, but tried to bring them to liberation and freedom.

The great heroes of our faith in South and Central America preached not just poverty but justice for the poor. They did not give credence to Marx's accusation that the message of the church—to endure poverty and injustice in this life because in the next they would go to heaven—was the opium of the people. The great Dom Helder Camara once said that when he fed the poor he was called a saint, and when he asked why they were poor he was called a communist.

Today's gospel asks us to look at our own lifestyle to see if it is consistent with the call of Jesus. Do we depend upon money and things for our fulfillment and happiness, or is the Lord first in all we do and in all we plan? Is it the Lord we worship or something else?

## Herod's Perplexity

LUKE 9:7-9

*Thursday of the Twenty-Fifth Week of the Year*

"Herod the tetrarch . . . was perplexed. . . . He was very curious to see Jesus."

Poor Herod had a golden opportunity. He was attracted to Jesus. Herod, who had John the Baptist beheaded because of a drunken oath to his wife's daughter, still had the possibility of finding life and forgiveness. There was still hope for Herod, the adulterer and murderer. Jesus would have gladly taken Herod into his arms and forgiven him, but Herod had too much baggage, too much of himself, his wealth, and his power invested in his life to put it all aside and follow Jesus. Yet, he theoretically could have done so if he really wanted to.

Perhaps we also have too much baggage to really allow Jesus into our hearts and lives. Maybe we feel that Jesus couldn't or wouldn't forgive our sins. Maybe we don't believe that the gift of life is not really meant for us but for someone else. Jesus is so willing and longing to give to Herod, to us, to anyone who will accept it, the gift of new life.

Like Herod, many are perplexed by Jesus and many are curious about Jesus. Many deeply admire Jesus but just can't find it in themselves to become his followers. So many look at Jesus from a distance—they love what they see and hear, but they are held back by so many things like guilt, fear, and their past.

But some are also made to feel unwelcome by the so-called followers of Christ. Many cannot fathom how those who claim to be the followers of Christ fail to live the gospel of Christ. They cannot understand how there can be injustice, violence, greed, ambition, and avarice in the church of the humble, poor man who came to serve and love all people. They remain on the edge of the church, like Karl Rahner's "anonymous Christian," because they cannot compromise their own integrity by joining followers of Christ who don't seem to live what they preach.

As Jesus calls and draws us closer, let us keep our eyes fixed only on him. Let us take his hand, and let us not look anywhere except into his loving eyes.

# Peter's Confession of Christ

### LUKE 9:18-22

*Friday of the Twenty-Fifth Week of the Year*

After Peter's profession of faith that Jesus is the Messiah of God, Jesus tells the apostles that it is not the right time to reveal this "secret" to all, and he also predicts the events of his own passion and suffering, his death and his resurrection.

There is a plan and destiny in the life of Jesus. All roads lead to Jerusalem and the cross. There is no denying it or avoiding it, and Jesus knows it only too well. He *must* go to Jerusalem. He *must* be crucified, but the Father will bring good from evil and life from death. Jesus places his life in his Father's hands. He trusts him. In the process of the journey there is much work to be done, and Jesus faithfully does the Father's will, day in and day out. In the great things and in the little things, he is totally obedient to the Father's call.

We do not know where the Father will lead us. We do not know what our Jerusalem will consist of. All that we know and can live is today. All that we are capable of is to put our lives in the hands of our loving Father. We can only trust in faith that God's love for us is perfect. God will always take care of us no matter where he leads us. God's grace will be sufficient, and God will always bring life from death.

As we die with Jesus in living out the Paschal Mystery, we believe and trust that we will rise with him. We know that in him is our victory and our salvation, that he will never abandon us or deny us. We trust that he will never lead where we will be overcome. We believe that his grace will always be sufficient.

Each day as we place ourselves in the hands of Jesus, we once again trust and believe that he will take care of us and that his grace will be all we require. His promise and his presence is why we can pray every day: "Thy will be done."

## The Prediction of the Passion

LUKE 9:43-45

*Saturday of the Twenty-Fifth Week of the Year*

"Pay close attention to what I tell you: The Son of Man must be delivered into the hands of men." The disciples failed to understand Jesus' warning.

It is simply terrifying and confusing to talk about or even think about the cross of Jesus. We spend so much energy trying to sanitize Christianity by removing, understating, or ignoring the cross. The problem is we just can't do it. If we try to get away without facing the cross in the life of Jesus, or in our own personal lives, we wind up with something nice—but it's not Christianity.

The idea of our faith is not to look for or rejoice in the cross. We never look for the cross for its own sake. The reality of Christ and Christianity is that in the lived daily life of the disciple of Jesus, there are events and moments in which we must give ourselves to something or someone greater than us. Some things are more important than our personal wants or comforts. In a "me" society, this kind of thinking is absurd. The spirit of today will tell us to seek what *we* enjoy and what *we* prefer.

We see this partially at least in the breakdown of marriage, family, priesthood, and religious life. We have forgotten how to, are emotionally unable to, live for and give our lives to other people. The ramifications this has for our world and society, as well as the church, are terrifying.

When we invite people to follow Jesus, we are inviting them to a lifestyle that takes delight in serving others and in living for and laying down one's life for others.

Marriage and parenthood are perfect imitations of the life of Christ. There is no such thing as marriage or parenthood without the intention to place the beloved first and to lay down one's life in service to them.

We cannot ever experience the joy, peace, contentment, and satisfaction that the Lord wants us to know without having first given the gift of ourselves to someone or something of value. As it has been said: "There's no crown without the cross." "There is no Easter without Good Friday." "Unless the grain of wheat falls into the earth and dies. . . ."

## Who Will Be the Greatest?

LUKE 9:46-50

*Monday of the Twenty-Sixth Week of the Year*

"Whoever welcomes this child welcomes me." In the summer of 1998, I had the great privilege of accompanying young people from my parish on a missionary retreat to El Salvador. We visited several orphanages in the country. It was a moving and life-challenging experience for all of us to be in this troubled but holy country.

I was moved again and again to tears as I saw the sisters who ran these orphanages and the love they had for these children, and the obvious love the children had for the sisters. The children who were abandoned, orphaned, and all in some way victims of the war, were truly Christ. As the sisters loved and cared for these children, they did it to Christ. Some of these sisters were in their seventies, yet their devotion and commitment to care for their little flocks were so moving and powerful that none of us from St. Brigid's could ever forget it. They had nothing, but they had everything.

The other incredible experience of Jesus was to see our young people as they loved and were present to these children. Most of us had lost our luggage, which contained gifts for the children. We were so disappointed we had nothing to give them. They quickly showed us we had everything to give—our love, our time, and our interest.

The beautiful people of El Salvador—especially the children—preached the gospel to us by loving us and allowing us to love them. When I saw my young people play, fool, eat, joke, play soccer in the blazing sun, sing, and dance with these children, I knew that Christ was powerfully present; and we all brought him home to the U.S.

Children lead us to God. The newborn baby has the power to teach the new parents to love as they never have before and to truly find God in the process. The growing child will be formed in the faith and love of its parents. When the ministries of caring and teaching the youth in our parishes are a real priority, the blessing of the Lord is truly upon us.

In the liturgy at Advent, we pray from Isaiah, "And a little child shall lead them." Every child is the Christ Child, leading us to a deeper and more profound experience of God's love. Let us take the hand of the child.

## Unwelcome by the Samaritan Town

LUKE 9:51-56

*Tuesday of the Twenty-Sixth Week of the Year*

The Samaritans will not welcome Jesus because he is on his way to Jerusalem. They are so caught up in their history of alienation from the Jewish people and their being ostracized by the Jewish people that they miss the chance of welcoming the Lord. Their past condemns them.

We can be just as blind and just as prejudiced as the Samaritans. Jesus is walking into our little towns awaiting a warm welcome from us, and often we are not able to see or hear him. We are too taken up with our worries, fears, hatreds, and our ingrained belief that nothing can really change in our lives. We sometimes believe that we are prisoners of our past and our actions and there is no way out. We are as "victimized" as the Samaritans, and we just don't think there is another chance for us.

If we would just allow Jesus in, things would be different. We can't change the past. We can't undo the history, but we can respond to the call and the possibility of the present. Even when we are responsible for the way things are, Jesus is still there to help us put the pieces together and begin again.

Living with AIDS can be an invitation to the closest relationship and walk with Jesus that we ever had. Putting our life together after a divorce is a holy time of responding as best we can to a new vocation. Single parenthood can be a new and glorious way of living in generosity and love as we devote our whole life and being to the well-being of our family. Accepting one's homosexuality becomes a great moment of grace as one truly is able to experience God's love in the way we have been created.

In all the monumental and difficult moments of life, Jesus comes to enter our village. Will we welcome him?

## Would-Be Followers of Jesus

LUKE 9:57-62

*Wednesday of the Twenty-Sixth Week of the Year*

Jesus makes it very clear in today's gospel that following him is an "all or nothing" affair. The three would-be disciples seem very open and willing to follow, and their requests seem quite reasonable. Yet, something is obviously holding them back from making that complete break with the past and embracing the new.

Quite frankly, I wonder if anyone is, or ever was, capable of making that total gift of the self to the Lord. Whether our call is to celibate or married commitment, Jesus is saying that we have to give everything. He is telling us not to hold back or go half way, but to give everything.

I am still struggling with what Jesus is asking of me. Material things don't seem quite the obstacle, rather wanting my own way; holding back love and service because I'm tired or afraid; having prejudices against certain people because of their theology; not giving myself in total generosity . . . there are so many ways in which I give him only part of myself.

But maybe giving a part is better than nothing. Maybe it's a beginning to a very long process of making the total gift of myself to the Lord. Maybe it is just that, a very long process in which I experience many deaths and resurrections, moving endings and new beginnings.

While I don't want to be complacent or mediocre, I must realize that I must grow into being that complete person in Jesus Christ. I must love the world and the beautiful things it offers; I must deepen relationships because it is there that the Lord is truly found. But in all of this, I must listen to the spirit of St. Benedict: "Prefer nothing to the love of Christ."

This gospel is a hard word that will take all of our lives to understand and to achieve, if indeed we ever can truly understand it or achieve it. Let's not be impatient about it.

# Jesus Sends the Seventy-Two

## LUKE 10:1-12

*Thursday of the Twenty-Sixth Week of the Year*

Jesus sends the seventy-two forth to proclaim the Kingdom. What we say now about vocations is what Jesus said so long ago: "The harvest is rich but the workers are few." Let's pray about the harvest and the need for workers, but not as we usually do.

When we talk about the remedy for the lack of vocations we usually go from the extremes of praying for vocations, speaking about the materialism of this world which prevents young people from making the commitment to radical service (as if marriage were not a radical commitment), to demanding that married men and women be allowed to be ordained. Let's not go in this direction. Let's reflect on our own personal call and vocation.

The heart of all vocations is baptism. In my entering the death and resurrection of Jesus Christ, I become an extension of his threefold role of priest, prophet, and king. We are all priests already. That is what baptism is all about. Sound theology can hold that in baptism, when we die and rise with Jesus, we are conformed to him. We are a new creation. Ordination calls forth or "ordains" what we already received in holy baptism.

There are going to be many political, theological, and power battles fought before the questions on holy orders are settled in the church. In the meantime, everyone must live out his or her priesthood.

We are all called to give life to those around us. We are all called to preach the gospel sometimes. (As St. Francis would say, "We may even use words.") We are all called to forgive sins—our own and others. We are all called to heal the sick in body, mind, and spirit. We are all called to celebrate the eucharist as we break the bread of life and love and give ourselves in loving commitment and service to one another.

Jesus did so few of the things that ordained priests do today. His priesthood, which was lived in loving service to others, is symbolized so powerfully in the washing of the feet. Isn't it time we all got our act together and started being priests? When we do so, all the politics and theology might just settle itself.

## Unrepentant Cities

LUKE 10:13-16

*Friday of the Twenty-Sixth Week of the Year*

I recently made a beautiful retreat at Mt. Savior Monastery in Elmira, New York. I always find it a life-giving and wonderful experience to enter into the life and daily prayer of the Benedictines. Part of their 1500-year-old charism is to bless and sanctify the day by gathering to sing the psalms and read scripture from before dawn to the end of the day. It is in this praising of the Lord at these different times that the deep and loving gratitude to the Lord for all his blessings is humbly expressed.

Poor Chorazin! Poor Bethsaida! They just didn't appreciate the blessing of the presence of Jesus among them. They did not stop to praise or thank him, they just went on with life and business as usual.

My visit to the monastery forced me to really pray the words of the psalms. I said, "I praise you" and "Thanks" so many times! The words began to affect my prayer as I began to praise him and thank him for all that he has done for me. I began to go back over the years and praise him for the love that was given to me in my family. My early years and growing up in beautiful Brooklyn were so wonderful. My parents, my grandparents, my sisters, relations, neighbors, the priests, the sisters, the brothers—everyone affirmed my goodness and helped me become a person.

My vocation as a priest, my parish families, my friends—all of them were beautiful experiences of God's love, and I thanked the Lord for them.

I also thanked him for the crosses and the times I didn't think I would survive. He sustained me and brought me through apparent death to new life and joy.

Lord, forgive me when I'm like these cities. You have given me so much. There is nothing I want or need. I am the most blessed man in the world, but I still don't act like it. I'm still like the two dead cities that do not know what they have. Forgive me, Lord, and help me to say "thank you" today.

## The Return of the Seventy-Two

LUKE 10:17-24

*Saturday of the Twenty-Sixth Week of the Year*

"You have revealed to the merest children." Something wonderful happened to the seventy-two disciples on the missionary journey, something incredible because they returned giving praise and jubilation to God. They returned happy. They returned like children. Jesus thanks his Father for what has been given to the seventy-two, and he calls them children. He makes the point to thank his Father that all these blessings and gifts were not given to the learned and wise, but to these children.

It's really hard to imagine what happened to change them so, but I do have a theory. When you have any small part in the coming of God's love into another ministry, it becomes intoxicating. When you look into someone's eyes and know that they have understood, seen, or been grasped by the Lord, you know that you are on holy ground. You know that the Lord has used you to speak and to touch another person. You also know that it was through no power of your own that God has acted, rather God has used you as a vessel and means to reach out to and heal another human being.

You become a person in deep awe and reverence because even though you know how wounded and limited you are, the Lord uses you to do powerful and glorious works in his name. Actually, the more aware you are of your limitations and sinfulness, the more the Lord is able to use you and the better vessel you become of his presence and love.

When you come to understand that you are totally incompetent and that everything is a gift of God, you can afford to begin to take on childlike qualities. When you have been allowed to handle the lightning rod of God's passionate love, you have no choice but to become giddy with the wine of joy. You have to sing and dance and play and do the things of a child because they are the only things that make any sense in the presence of the Great Lover.

The less seriously we take ourselves and the more joy that fills the church, the closer we are to being the children of the loving Father.

## The Parable of the Good Samaritan

LUKE 10:25-37

*Monday of the Twenty-Seventh Week of the Year*

"Go and do the same." The Samaritan whom history has named "good" is presented by Jesus as a model of what love, compassion, and mercy are in practical and everyday life.

As Jesus tells this story of the plight of the poor man who fell victim to robbers, he makes many points that we have to reflect on. The first was that those who should have stopped didn't. The priest and the Levite and the religious professionals saw the beaten man lying there and passed on.

It reminds us that just because we have a title and a place of honor in the church doesn't mean that we always live up to it. Just because we are practicing Catholics in terms of keeping the law and fulfilling our obligations doesn't necessarily mean that we are growing in the love of God and neighbor. That requires a constant and ongoing process of conversion.

It is not unusual for very "religious" people to be racist and prejudicial. The call to conversion is the call to grow more deeply in our relationship of love with God, our neighbor, and ourselves. We must never allow religious practice and business to ever become a smoke screen that prevents us or excuses us from seeking God.

The Samaritan, on the other hand, is an outcast. He's not in the mainstream of Jewish religious life. He's despised. But he is the one whose basic humanity breaks through. He can't walk by a wounded man and not help him. His religion is not the kind that finds itself expressed in a church; it is the religion of the heart based on an innate appreciation and respect for humanity.

Jesus is making a very strong point to his hearers, and they won't miss the sting of his story. Of course, it doesn't have to be "either/or"—either religious or authentically holy. It should be "both/and" for us! Yet there is caution: Don't hide behind religion to absolve you from the more important things and don't ever underestimate the holiness of many who are not part of the "club."

# Martha and Mary

## LUKE 10:38-42

*Tuesday of the Twenty-Seventh Week of the Year*

Martha and Mary and their brother, Lazarus, were very special friends of Jesus. He found great peace and deep friendship in their home. Jesus will call Lazarus from the grave, and Martha and Mary will become the symbols of the two parts of the Christian heart. Martha will be the symbol of the active life and Mary of the contemplative life. Their special graces are lived out in the church in the dedicated lives of active religious and contemplative religious.

But Martha and Mary symbolize the hearts and the lives of each and every Christian. We are all called to be contemplatives, and we are all called to work hard to build up the Kingdom.

The art of the Christian life is our relationship with Jesus. Our deep, real, and life-giving love of Jesus is the most important part of our life. We are called to cultivate it and deepen it each day of our life. We have to sit at the feet of Jesus to listen and be silent in the presence of the Lord. Whether we are married, single, divorced, priest, or religious, we cannot live the life of Christ as it is meant to be lived without that space and time in which Jesus touches and heals our hearts.

Yet, the "Mary" in our hearts cannot be allowed to become lazy, self-absorbed, or forgetful of the people around us. Our contemplation must lead to action. We are empowered to be able "to do."

Just as the church needs pray-ers, it also needs workers. It needs Marthas! What a blessing Marthas are to a home or parish! How wonderful it is to be with people who are not lazy and who will go out of their way to help and lend a hand. Some homes are like being in heaven because they are made happy and joyful places by the loving labor of parents.

It is such a blessing to be with hard working and dedicated people. They inspire and challenge us to be the best we can. The only caution to the Marthas is that they don't wear themselves out with work. They need to take care of themselves. Jesus is interested in the long haul. The Marthas also have to be careful that in their business and hard work they do not fail to make time for the care of the soul and spirit. They also have to make time for prayer so that they will know why they are doing the beautiful things they do.

## The Lord's Prayer

LUKE 11:1-4

*Wednesday of the Twenty-Seventh Week of the Year*

"Lord, teach us to pray as John taught his disciples."

The response of Jesus is history. The Lord's Prayer is in the heart of every Christian. It is a prayer we speak in times of joy and in times of fear. It is the universal prayer of all Christians. It is the ecumenical prayer uniting his disciples of every church and community. It is a prayer of profound emotion when sung with hands joined. It is truly the first prayer of the church.

Each phrase of the Lord's Prayer is filled with such profound theological and spiritual meaning. Each phrase can be studied and meditated upon and never be totally understood or grasped. This prayer is scripture, the inspired word of God. It must be prayed in such great faith and love.

The first phrase really is the whole prayer. To understand that is to understand all there is to know: "Our Father." Jesus is leading us into a whole new way of looking upon our God. He tells us that God is Father. He teaches us that we will best relate to God when we accept him as the loving parent. All that we know in human terms of parenthood helps us to understand at least in some small way that God's love for us is as passionate, ferocious, and all-consuming as the love of a mother or father for their child.

There is nothing a mother or father will not do for their child. They will willingly die for their flesh and blood if that is necessary. They will do anything to provide for the well-being and health of their child. Their child's life and well-being is the very driving force of their life. Nothing is more important.

And so we say "Our Father," and we cannot believe how God loves us as flesh of his flesh and bone of his bone. His love for us is all-consuming. His love is the very meaning of our lives. His love will be expressed to us in the ultimate gift, the gift of his Son, Jesus Christ, as our brother and Savior.

We are made one family as we pray together with the whole world: "Our Father."

## More Teachings on Prayer

LUKE 11:5-13

*Thursday of the Twenty-Seventh Week of the Year*

We continue yesterday's request to the Lord: "Teach us how to pray."

Yesterday's response of Jesus in teaching us the Lord's Prayer is so solemn, holy, and moving. Today continues Jesus' answer by telling a great and funny story that must cross the best of theologians because it is not so "theological." It's just true. Not only that, it works!

Jesus describes his Father as the father of a family who has retired for the evening. They are all wrapped up in their blankets and rugs. The doors are locked, and they're all set for a long winter's nap.

Then it comes. Bang, bang, bang—"Please open the door! I just got unexpected company and I have nothing to serve them. Please give me some bread. Please help me out."

The father nicely but firmly tells the friend that they're all in bed and he can't help him out. The friend won't take "no" for an answer and keeps banging on the door until his friend wakes up the whole family and all the animals. He gives him all he wants just to shut him up and get rid of him.

The moral of the story is obvious. Drive God crazy. Be persistent. Don't stop asking. Keep it up until you get what you want. As I said, the theology of all this is questionable. All I know is that it works! God wants to be bothered. God wants us to ask, and our prayers are very important to God. We should never hesitate to ask for what we need and even for what we just want. Jesus has told us so and we better do as he says: "How much more will the heavenly Father give the Holy Spirit to those who ask him." The Father will answer in the way that is best for us. Just don't stop asking. Remember his love for you, that you are precious to him and that he will always care for you, his beloved child.

"Ask and you shall receive; seek and you shall find; knock and it shall be opened to you."

## Jesus and Beelzebub

LUKE 11:15-26

*Friday of the Twenty-Seventh Week of the Year*

"He casts out the devils by the power of Beelzebub." It is not unusual for holiness and love to be accused of being sin and hate. Yet that is what the crowd is actually saying about Jesus! What a dreadful and terrible thing to see those for whom Jesus has come to totally turn their backs on him and miss the very point of who and what he is, the Father's love incarnate.

It is not unusual for goodness to be called evil and evil to design itself as good, "an angel of light." So many of the martyrs of Central and South America were depicted as devils wanting to destroy church and state when all they were doing was working for the basic human rights of the people. Dom Helder Camara said that when he fed the poor he was called a saint. When he asked why they were poor he was called a communist.

We are called to follow the light. That is our guidance and our hope. We can only discern by the presence of the fruits of the Holy Spirit.

We can only call good, good and evil, evil. We say "yes" when we mean "yes" and "no" when we mean "no." In the coming of truth we open to God's call and presence. We can only be people of truth by being truthful to ourselves and saying and doing only those things that we personally believe in, things we live for and things that we would die for.

The disciple of Jesus living for and motivated by love can expect, as was the Lord, to be called evil. The disciple must be completely sure of who they are and why they do what they do. In that leaven of truth that is the heart, the disciple must know that they are walking with the Lord and that they are truly the Lord's friend.

What happens around us might be very destructive and violent. It is in the core of our being that the peace of Christ dwells and we know that we are doing his holy will.

# Blessedness

LUKE 11:27-28

*Saturday of the Twenty-Seventh Week of the Year*

"Blest are they who hear the word of God and keep it."

Those who have deep devotion to Mary don't like this gospel because it seems to be a put-down of Mary. A woman from the crowd shouts out, "Blest is the womb that bore you and the breasts that nursed you!" And Jesus turned it all around and made a Kingdom statement: "Blest are they who hear the word of God and keep it."

Jesus is telling his hearers that to be part of the Kingdom is greater than even the bonds of love between a mother and her child, even when the child is the Christ himself! Being a part of the Kingdom is the new creation.

No matter how low or great our place might be, we all have free access to the Kingdom as we hear the word of God and live its beautiful call to be part of the new creation. Power, position, or birth can't buy our way into the Kingdom. We enter into the Kingdom by wanting to be the Lord's disciples, by hearing and accepting his word with love and joy, and by living it with all our hearts.

Jesus calls and invites each of us by name. No one has an "inside track"; all are equal at the banquet table of the Kingdom of God. In God's house all have perfect equality. The only prerequisite is faith and love.

As Jesus calls us, we have to know how much he loves us. Our election to be part of the Kingdom is part of this incredible mystery of God's love. Why has he loved us so? Why are we so precious to him? One of the great joys of heaven will be to understand more and more the depth of love that God has for us in Christ Jesus the Lord.

We are his masterpiece and his beloved. He has made us a little less than God. His delight is for us to be with him and love him always.

As true as all of this is, I still think Mary gave Jesus a piece of her mind when he got home that night and reminded him that "Kingdom or no Kingdom, you only have one mother!" I know mine would!

## The Sign of Jonah

LUKE 11:29-32

*Monday of Twenty-Eighth Week of the Year*

Jesus confronts his listeners with this hard cold truth: they cannot truly see him or hear his message because they are looking for the extraordinary. They want signs and wonders, and all Jesus has to offer is himself. Jesus is speaking a word to them that has the power to bring life, meaning, and peace, but these poor people are only interested in the circuses and bread that they think Jesus will provide. They want the extraordinary, but they fail to realize that the incarnate God is only available to us in the ordinary experiences of daily life.

Nothing much has changed. So many are still going all over the world with the hope of finding the God who is no farther away than in our own hearts. Many still look for the special prayer, the special devotion, or the special place to find God. While these things may be good in themselves, they will only lead us back to our own hearts.

Where is our God? Where can we find God? Our God dwells in our hearts. We have been baptized into the very life of the Father, Son, and the Holy Spirit. Holiness comes to us when we can acknowledge the presence of the living God within us, and adore, serve, and love God. We do not make God present by long prayers and fasting. God is there . . . always. God never leaves us. Our call is to acknowledge and claim for ourselves that divine presence which is within us and will never leave us.

Our God is present in all of our relationships. To love God is to love our dear families and friends. The covenant of our love with the Lord is deepened as we give ourselves in deeper commitment and love to our spouse, children, parents, siblings, and friends. *God's* love is experienced in *their* love.

Our God is present when we reach out and touch the poor. There are so many kinds of poverty in the world. When we touch someone, especially the broken, suffering, and poor, we touch the Lord.

We find God not in great signs and wonders. We find God in ourselves and all around us in the ordinary things of life.

## Purification Inside and Outside

LUKE 11:37-41

*Tuesday of the Twenty-Eighth Week of the Year*

Jesus is doing again what he seems to do best—eating and drinking with people. Jesus enters into the community of their homes so that he will have the opportunity to share with them on a deep level of friendship and intimacy. Eating and drinking with someone is a very holy activity for Jesus and his contemporaries. It is truly a prelude to the communion he will have with us and for all of us in the sacrament of the eucharist.

Jesus takes his place at the table. He sits down with people he hopes will become his friends. He makes himself vulnerable and available, and he takes advantage of the opportunity to teach. At this particular dinner party Jesus uses the reaction of the hosts and guests to his nonobservance of the rules of washing. They are scandalized that he is not concerned with purification.

Jesus is very strong in challenging his audience about their following external observance while forgetting about and neglecting internal purity. Jesus is very hard with this group. He must know a lot about them. He must know that they need to be challenged to leave their safe and legalistic religion and begin to be concerned with things of the heart. He is challenging the underpinnings of their religious faith by telling them what they think is important (the external) is unimportant; that what they neglect (the internal) is what really counts.

There's a lot of the Pharisee in all of us as we construct our own religion that thrives on the externals while we easily overlook what truly matters—truth, mercy, justice, forgiveness, and love.

Jesus calls his disciples to a religion of the heart, one flowing from the spirit of the gospels and freed from false religion of the external and the legalistic.

Let us pray for ourselves and for our church that we be a people of the loving truth striving to follow Jesus in all the demands of the heart. It is hard to let go of what is safe. When we enter into the area of the heart with Jesus, we find it to be a challenging, even frightening place, but it is where we find God. It is well worth the journey.

## Jesus Denounces the
## Pharisees and Lawyers

LUKE 11:42-46

*Wednesday of the Twenty-Eighth Week of the Year*

When the apostles heard Jesus speaking his "woes" to the scribes, Pharisees, and lawyers, they probably looked at one another and said, "What side of the bed did he get up on today?" Jesus is angry, and he is not missing a great opportunity to tell his hearers what he thinks of formalized, external religion that takes the place of the religion of the heart.

The Pharisees are "woed" because they pay their tithe but neglect the more basic demands of justice and love. In reality, there can never be any true religion as long as we tolerate injustice. We are not doing a holy thing when we give food and money to someone whose basic human rights are denied but do nothing to obtain this person's rights.

Archbishop Camara was called a communist because when he fed the poor he asked them why they were poor in the first place. People like Archbishop Camara, Archbishop Romero, and many of the other saints of Latin America call the church to something far greater than charity—they call the church to justice.

The Pharisees are "wooed" because they seek prestige, status, and places of honor. The true disciples of the Lord are delighted to be servants and to take the lowest place. They imitate the Master who shows us what real greatness is by washing the feet of the lowliest. The model of ministry that Jesus gives to us is not power but service.

Finally, the lawyers are "wooed" along with all the other so-called ministers who instead of lifting the burdens of their people, heap greater ones on their shoulders, and are hard and cold to the pain of those who come to them in need.

## The Key of Knowledge

LUKE 11:47-54

*Thursday of the Twenty-Eighth Week of the Year*

Jesus continues in today's gospel to test the lawyers. We have to be careful to remember that we're not off the hook just because we may not be lawyers. Jesus is not speaking so much about a profession but a way of thinking and living.

Jesus condemns them for taking up the key of knowledge. They not only fail to enter into the house of knowledge, but also prevent those whom they teach from entering. That's a very serious charge.

It's really about the responsibility that leaders have to seek and to share the truth. We who are the teaching and evangelistic ministers of the church are meant to lead all people to the truth—to God. The church is meant to be the first guardian and seeker of the truth. All too often it is not. It sometimes doesn't trust its people to seek the truth in honesty, and it sets up all kinds of defenses of censorship and condemnation.

How many theologians in our own day have been treated unjustly by church institutions seeking out heresy! How many times has the church resorted to dishonesty to protect itself or its teachings, believing that anything justifies defending the faith!

It is so difficult for the church to admit its errors or personal guilt. Thank God Pope John Paul II has led the church into this millennium with his *mea culpa* for the sins and abuses of the church in the past.

It is so hard for us to say, "I was wrong" or "I am sorry." When we do say these words, we lift heavy burdens and bring peace and light to places in our own hearts where there was darkness. Jesus calls us to a very pure and transparent life—let us not be afraid of the key to knowledge. Let us use it well to speak and to live the truth.

# Warnings and Encouragement

## LUKE 12:1-7

*Friday of the Twenty-Eighth Week of the Year*

In today's gospel, Jesus first looks at his disciples and speaks, and then to the vast crowd who have come to hear and see him.

Jesus speaks to the disciples and to all leaders about the "yeast" of the Pharisees, which is hypocrisy. Ever since, the Lord has been warning us about that hypocrisy whenever we read the gospels. Yeast is what makes the dough rise. It gives the loaf its size and shape and texture. If the yeast of the church is humility, compassion, and mercy, then the church is the attractive, welcoming, living bread inviting all people to come and sup and be nourished. If the yeast is hypocrisy, then the church is the untruthful and power-hungry institution that is cold and unwelcoming. When the yeast of hypocrisy reigns, the leadership of the church ceases to be the role model and mentor of what discipleship truly means, and it becomes the cold and hard ruler placing heartless burdens on people.

So many times Jesus calls the church to truthfulness and authenticity. He calls us to walk in the light and never to fear the dark because we have nothing to be afraid of.

It is always such a great temptation for those who lead large religious organizations such as schools, dioceses, and parishes to become too engrossed in ministry. Religious institutions often deliver a "product" which is in itself very good, but sometimes forget that the most important "product," from the leader on down, is a humble, honest, truthful, and loving Christian who each day opens his or her heart to the Lord in simple and humble prayer.

Sometimes the leaven of us new Pharisees is that we become fanatic "ministers" who deliver a marvelous product but spend too much energy and time on the product and not really enough on becoming and being a Christian.

I sometimes think that I am a much better minister than Christian. Do you know the feeling?

## Acknowledging Jesus

LUKE 12:8-12

*Saturday of the Twenty-Eighth Week of the Year*

Jesus tells us today that he will acknowledge before the angels of God anyone who acknowledges him before others. What does it mean to *acknowledge*? It means to profess, confess, recognize, accept, or own up to. It means far more than the profession of a creedal statement about Jesus Christ. It really means acknowledging *who* Jesus Christ is and *what* he has done in our life. Jesus Christ is acknowledged when we recognize, respect, and embrace him in all of our sisters and brothers—especially the poor, the suffering, and the unloved.

We do a wonderful job in reciting all the glories of Jesus Christ in the creed every Sunday. We bow and kneel as we acknowledge his presence in the blessed sacrament. We venerate and profess the word of God, the sacred scripture, as it is proclaimed liturgically. We wonderfully acknowledge the Lord Jesus for what he is—the God-Man.

We acknowledge him under the appearance of bread and wine. We hear him in the words of scripture. We praise him in our creeds and prayers.

Yet, we have a big problem in acknowledging him or professing him where it really counts—in the flesh and blood of our fellow men and women. Jesus is the homeless man, the youth on drugs, the girl who just had an abortion, the divorced person, the single parent, the woman dying of cancer, the addicted teenager, the alcoholic, the person dying of AIDS. Jesus Christ is all of humanity in its beauty, its glory, and in its agony.

When we acknowledge Jesus in all of these sisters and brothers, when we reach out to them in love and compassion, he acknowledges us before the angels. Jesus is in the holy sacrament, Jesus is in the scriptures, but most of all he is in the least of his sisters and brothers. When we find him in them we will never lose him.

## The Parable of the Rich Fool

LUKE 12:13-21

*Monday of Twenty-Ninth Week of the Year*

"You fool! This very night your life shall be required of you." We all get into the habit of building new barns in which to store all our possessions. We all want security. We want to possess. We want to have something to fall back on come that rainy day.

The young used to be so detached from material goods. Advertising, TV, and other media have succeeded in making the young just as greedy as the old. The lie of being only as good as you look or what you own has been swallowed hook, line, and sinker.

Jesus in today's gospel tries to reverse the tide by telling us the story of the rich man who fills his new barns with all his crops and wealth. He has made the accumulation of things the goal of his life. It is not that the things are bad in themselves, it is his heart that is out of tune, for he feels that the things mean more than anything else.

"You fool!" What a cruel thing to have to hear about your whole life's work. Tonight the rich man dies, and who gets his wealth and all that he has given his youth, dreams, marriage, family, and God to achieve?

The Lord invites us to grow rich in the sight of God. What makes us rich in God's sight? There is another

"Trinity" to guide our lives and make us rich in God's eyes: truth, integrity, and love.

When we walk in God's truth we are transparent. We speak and live God's truth in all the areas of our lives. We never fear the light because we are people of the light. We never hide from anyone or anything.

Truth leads to integrity and integrity flows from truth. It is the living of our lives in honesty. It is choosing the right in all things just because it is right. It is living by following a conscience formed by prayer and one's relationship to the Lord.

Charity, or love, sums up all of life. Love is being rich in the sight of God. Love calls us to respect and honor every human being, and it demands that we never deliberately hurt or offend another human being.

When we fill our barns with the virtues and the love of God, then they are full of God's blessings and we are truly rich in God's sight.

## Watchfulness

LUKE 12:35-38

*Tuesday of the Twenty-Ninth Week of the Year*

"Let your belts be fastened around your waists and your lamps be burning ready." The Lord is telling us we've got to be ready for his return. We can't be procrastinators or put it off until we're ready.

Delay and procrastination in the spiritual life is a very real problem. Usually it follows a scenario like this: we are deluged with work, responsibilities, and stressed out—so much so that we don't have the time or the energy to pray, reflect, or rest. We are on the go all the time, doing great and wonderful things, but we don't have the space or time to be present to the One for whom we do all of it in the first place. Instead of our work, life, and ministry flowing from the depth of our relationship with

Jesus, we are always promising ourselves that when things get back to "normal," we'll find the time to be with and speak to the One for whom we live.

We wouldn't think about spending a day without drinking, eating, and sleeping. Not to do so is crazy, like not having time to get gas when we're out driving. I can honestly say that most of the best, holiest, and most dedicated people I know will confess to not making time to pray, being too busy to pray, or excusing themselves with the promise that when things get back to normal, they'll get back on the track. I don't know about you, but I have never had a normal day, and my prayer life, like my dieting, exercising, and reading, is always "tomorrow!"

We just can't afford to procrastinate. We have to have a peace about us that comes only from order. For starters, do we have a daily schedule? Have we set aside time on our daily schedule for prayer, reading, study, exercise, recreation, and work?

A spiritual director is very important for us to set reasonable goals and objectives. It just is so obvious what we have to do. Why do we resist common sense? Take out a piece of paper and pen and make your schedule. Let it revolve around the time of your prayer. Let it be the heart of your life and everything else will fall in its proper place.

## Watchful Servants

LUKE 12:39-48

*Wednesday of the Twenty-Ninth Week of the Year*

I don't know how reverent it is for him to do it, but Jesus compares himself to a thief in the night. The moral? "You better be ready because you don't know when I'm coming to take you home to heaven or send you to the other place." Are *you* ready to die right here and now? Am I?

What a pointed and uncomfortable question that is. "I'll be ready after I do this or that. I'll go with you when I've spoken to this one and made peace with that one."

"No!" says the Lord. "I want you now." I'm not ready. How about you? The thought of dying terrifies us most when we have failed to live and love. When we haven't given our life and love to anyone or anything, death always is too soon. It is painful to leave this beautiful world. It is painful to leave those we have loved, but when we've lived a life of love we have already been in heaven here on earth. Heaven and hell are right here among us. It is what we have created by our choices and decisions.

The person who lives in love is always ready for Jesus' return. No matter that Jesus comes like that thief in the night; he will find that person at any time of the day or night doing the same thing—loving.

The loving may be commuting to work. It may be bathing the children or teaching a class or reading a book. It doesn't matter what the person of love is doing. It is all the same—it is loving. The concern of this person is not when will Jesus come; it will only be, "How can I love more and serve Jesus more faithfully?"

## Jesus: A Cause of Division

LUKE 12:49-53

*Thursday of the Twenty-Ninth Week of the Year*

Jesus wants to set the world on fire with his love. He wants to kindle this great fire that will bring his warmth, life, and love to all people. He wants no one to be cold or alone. He wants to kindle a revolution that will transform this world by love and mercy.

The irony of this is that the Kingdom of love will not always bring with it the gift of peace for those who proclaim it and preach it. The testimony of the events of our times shows that some of the great peacemakers did not always experience peace themselves, but persecution and even death itself. Romero, Camara, the Salvadoran women, and Jesuits—the list is long and stained in blood.

Love sometimes brings hate; peace sometimes evokes persecution; and justice for the poor can bring the enmity of the rich and religious. Those who work for peace and justice are very likely not to enjoy a great deal of peace.

Even the church, which under Pope John Paul II and his predecessors has a wonderful record of defending human rights, sometimes is uncomfortable and doesn't understand those who have a passion for justice for all. Traditionally, the church has centered upon saving souls while sometimes neglecting saving the whole person by achieving their full potential as human beings.

Karl Marx said that religion was the opium of the people, meaning that the promise of heaven is like a drug preventing us from facing the pain and the agony of the poor. We neglect the agony of this world with the promise of the happiness of heaven.

Those who questioned this philosophy made a lot of enemies because they were questioning the status quo. This meant that there would have to be change, and change is always resisted.

That is why those who work for justice often do not experience peace in this world. They experience divisions and pain. They become the martyrs in whose blood comes a new redemption and life. They pay dearly for the establishment of the new Kingdom of peace and justice, the Kingdom of God on earth.

# Interpreting the Times

*Friday of the Twenty-Ninth Week of the Year*

Jesus would have made a great meteorologist. He knew how to predict the weather. In this interesting gospel, Jesus is basically saying to the crowds: if you can predict the weather and know when it will rain because of clouds rising in the west and when it will be hot because of the winds from the south, why can't you read the signs of the times and know what is happening before your very eyes?

In many ways we are like that crowd to which Jesus spoke. We know so many things, and we are accomplished in so many skills. Why do we not know the basics and the important things for our happiness and well-being?

We all have been given so many gifts and the blessing of our tradition. The scriptures and the eucharist and two thousand years of our tradition are available to each and every one of us. But we sometimes don't look there. We look elsewhere for our truth and life and neglect all the Lord wants us to have.

Sometimes the most learned and clever can't see or hear what the Lord is offering to us. When we become too sophisticated and too wise to be humble disciples, we look for guidance and wisdom in the wrong places. How common it is for wonderful and holy men and women who lead the church not to have a real spiritual life. They admit that they don't have time to pray. It is no wonder that their lives and ministry often have no soul or joy; they have deprived themselves of the joy and consolation of letting Jesus love them in daily prayer.

How is your prayer life? Is there some time carved out of your schedule each day that belongs to only Jesus? Do you have a daily appointment with Jesus so that you can experience his love, guidance, tenderness, and challenge each day?

All the degrees in the world, all of the most wonderful talents and gifts will never equal what Jesus will do for you in the quiet time of your daily personal prayer time. It is the most important thing we will ever do. It will color, direct, and transform everything we are and do.

As we all try to be the most proficient and best equipped person for our work, let's not forget what is as obvious as the clouds in the sky and the gentle wind: we cannot live without Jesus. We cannot give to others someone we don't personally know ourselves.

## Repent or Perish

LUKE 13:1-9

*Saturday of the Twenty-Ninth Week of the Year*

Today's gospel begins in a harsh way as Jesus calls us to repentance and warns us that we will perish if we don't change our hearts. Jesus tells us that we cannot allow evil to rule our lives and that we have to be serious and conscientious about our daily journey to conversion.

The lesson is softened with the beautiful story of the fig tree that has not given fruit in three years. The master orders the gardener to cut it down. Why waste good soil on a tree that gives no fruit?

But the gardener pleads with the master to allow him to dig around the tree, water it, and fertilize it and thus maybe next year the tree will bear fruit.

I am in awe and thanksgiving of the mercy and love of God when I realize how many years the Lord has been patient with me for not giving fruit. How merciful and how patient God is! The year of cultivating and manuring and watering has extended itself for decades, and I still delay in giving the Lord the fruit of pure loving faith and devotion he deserves.

And still he waits. Still he cultivates. Still he waters. How kind and merciful God has been to me. God has never given up and has never revoked his call and love. The love and mercy of God to me has been unlimited. It has been a very long "year" with no end in sight, and yet he waits and waits and never gives up on me.

I know my experience is your experience my dear reader. In the face of the patient and loving God, maybe all God really is asking of us is that we be patient with one another. Perhaps God is asking us to have the same compassion with those in our lives as God has with us. As we contemplate our own personal imperfection, maybe we can become a bit more tolerant of the imperfection of others in our lives.

"Leave it to another year." "Give him another chance." Thank God for the mercy that knows no limit. Rejoice in that mercy and share it with our sisters and brothers.

## Jesus Heals a Crippled Woman

### LUKE 13:10-17

*Monday of the Thirtieth Week of the Year*

Today we see in the gospel the beautiful scene of Jesus curing the woman who had been possessed by a demon for eighteen years. The description of the poor woman is heart-rending: "She was badly stooped—quite incapable of standing erect." What a vivid description of the power of evil in our lives!

So many people are bent over and dragged down by so many personal and societal evils. People who have not been loved as they should have; people who have been abused, hurt, put down or ignored all their lives; people who have suffered in unhappy marriages . . . the list is endless of the things in our world that drag people down so that they literally cannot stand up straight.

Into this woman's life walks Jesus who lays his hand upon her, and she stands up straight for the first time. How wonderful to see a person stand up and be proud of who they are! Our mothers knew what they were talking about when they told us: "Stand straight!"

The church's mission is to touch the world with the love of Jesus so that everyone will experience the joy of respecting and honoring themselves, and thus be able to stand up straight. What a holy thing we do when we encourage and affirm children so that they are happy with themselves and can stand up straight.

The church is called to take off people's shoulders the burdens of guilt. The church is meant to set people free to lead them into the love of God and the world. The church is called to help lift the burdens and pain of sin and poor choices of the past. The church, which is us, is meant to be the healer and the reconciler of all people.

When we are bent over by the events and experiences of life, we hear the call and the invitation of Jesus to come to him. He wants to lift our burdens. He wants to be there for us. His mercy and love is not just meant for others; it is meant for us. He loves us so much and we mean so much to him.

Isn't it strange that those who so often lead others to Christ are so reluctant to go to him themselves? Sometimes those who speak so beautifully of the mercy of God are hesitant to believe that that mercy is meant for them.

We would all be such better ministers of love and healing if we would allow Jesus to raise us up.

# The Parables of the Mustard Seed and the Yeast

## LUKE 13:18-21

*Tuesday of the Thirtieth Week of the Year*

Today Jesus speaks to us about faith. He compares it to the mustard seed and the yeast. If anyone wants to see what faith is really like, he or she must spend time in a parish community. The experiences of faith that I have been privileged to witness have changed me and the way I think, judge, and live my life.

In a parish community one meets people who are deeply immersed in lives of prayer. When I become aware of the prayer life of very simple people, it humbles me. There are so many ordinary people who are in real and constant communion with God. Their call in faith and their response is as real and powerful as any of the great men and women called by God in scriptures. They know the Lord in a deep and profound way.

The mustard seed of faith grows into the strong and life-giving tree of faith. As I see families bear unspeakable pain and stress in the illness and suffering of family members, I know that it is God who sustains them. There have been incidents of tragedy and death in the parish when the faith and love of special families deeply touched the entire parish and brought us all closer to God and to one another.

The community has gathered around the coffin of very special ones whom we all knew to be saints. Their funerals were actually canonizations by the people. We knew where they were, and we rejoiced that they would always be in our hearts.

Faith changes everything. What a blessing it is. What a gift of God! It is also a great responsibility. Faith must be the leaven in the community. It must give life to all. It must raise up all to a higher and more beautiful life in Christ.

To be gifted by faith is a special call to transform a family, a friend, a spouse, or a parish. It is the duty of the blessed and gifted to share their blessings and gifts with the whole community.

Let us ask our Lord for a deeper faith so that we may become the instruments of his healing, life, and grace in our families and communities. Once the seed is planted it will never stop growing. It will be the yeast that will transform everything in this world.

## The Narrow Door

LUKE 13:22-30

*Wednesday of the Thirtieth Week of the Year*

Today's gospel is somber in that it touches on salvation and the need of walking in the way of the Lord. Jesus advises us to come in through the narrow door. This means pulling ourselves together. We can't enter through the narrow door if we're laden down with many burdens and carry many objects. The image of the narrow door calls us to a true sense of reform and change of heart.

We can't grasp on to Jesus and the things of this world at the same time. We know that our spiritual journey always includes getting rid of things that we don't need, especially things that are not good for us and that distract us and weigh us down.

The narrow door reminds us of purity of heart. It tells us that we can't serve two masters. We cannot belong to Jesus and be possessed by things. Our God *is* a jealous God. God demands the totality of our hearts and our love. The Lord cannot be one of many pleasant "gods" and distractions that make our life bearable. God is God. We always need to smash the false gods of ego, possessions, and pleasure so that there can be only the one true God who commands our whole being.

God forbid that when we come knocking at the door to enter the Kingdom, the Lord says what he said to those in today's gospel: "I tell you, I do not know where you come from. Away from me, you evildoers!"

As we approach the end of the liturgical year, the Lord will tell us even more clearly that we must be prepared. We must be ready. Our hearts must be disposed to embrace the Lord. Nothing must be in them that can distract us from loving and serving the one great treasure—Jesus, the Lord.

## The Lament Over Jerusalem

### LUKE 13:31-35

*Thursday of the Thirtieth Week of the Year*

"I must proceed on course . . . no prophet can be allowed to die anywhere except in Jerusalem." There's no fudging here. Jesus knows where he's going, and he's determined to go. I wonder if Herod ever found out that Jesus called him a fox—not a flattering title. The fox is the one who breaks into the chicken coop to kill and destroy those who are defenseless.

Jesus is obviously not afraid of Herod or anyone else. His life is to do the will of the Father and proceed on the course laid out for him. He will not reconsider. He will not change his mind. He will not compromise.

How about us? Do we follow the path of our vocation, or do we get too comfortable? Does everything become too ordinary? Do we lose the sharpness and the passion?

Most of the great renewal movements in the church have had the same purpose: to renew and kindle the spark. Whether it is Marriage Encounter, Cursillo, RENEW 2000 . . . they all mean to do the same things—

light the fire and let it blaze. They get us back on track so that we turn our head to our Jerusalem and keep going.

It's not always easy to keep going. It's not always easy to keep the spark of priesthood, marriage, religious life, friendship, etc. alive. We heed the moment and occasions that renew and give us new life and new enthusiasm.

There is no greater blessing than to see a priest or nun really happy and alive in his or her vocation. Often we encounter sad and tired, but very good people, who need to be renewed and affirmed as life-giving in their holy calling. There's nothing as life-giving to the church than to see a married couple deeply in love with each other and being beautiful and loving parents. When I walk into a home filled with that kind of love, I know that I stand on holy ground and that I am in God's presence.

When Jesus weeps over Jerusalem, maybe he's weeping for his dear friends whom he has called by name to do wonderful things like raise families, minister to his people, and proclaim the Kingdom. Perhaps he weeps because we don't care for our hearts as we should; or that we do not allow him to love and nurture us as we should. Jesus doesn't just call us to walk to Jerusalem; he promises to be there to help us on our way.

## Jesus Heals the Man With Dropsy

LUKE 14:1-6

*Friday of the Thirtieth Week of the Year*

"They kept silent after Jesus asked them if it were lawful to cure on the sabbath." Jesus must respond to the need of the man with dropsy. He reaches out, heals the man, and sends him on his way. There is no question about it: the law of love far outweighs the law of tradition. It will be just such actions on the part of Jesus that seem to contradict the law that will lead him to the cross.

How easy it is to keep the law and do what is correct, even if it means not doing what is right. It is a fine art and all too common to use the law to get away without doing what God really wants of us.

Don't let yourself be duped by a feeling of righteousness when you know you are not doing what God really expects of you. Don't hide behind canon law to be excused from doing what the Lord wants you to do in concrete cases where charity demands much more of you.

When we study the life and death of Oscar Romero, we see his witness and preaching, and eventually his death, as one of the most powerful witnesses of our times to the gospel of Jesus. He might have been "prudent" and stayed within the directives and wishes of the governments of El Salvador, the United States, and the Vatican. He could not. He was called to something much more demanding—he had to embrace his suffering people; he had to name evil for what it was; and he had to imitate the example of Jesus, the Good Shepherd, in laying down his life for his beloved people.

He could have played it safe, be alive today, and be a cardinal. He did not; he could not. He had to reach out, touch, and heal his people—especially on the sabbath.

When we see a similarity in someone's life to that of Jesus, we know they are on the right track. When we at least in some small way live the beatitude, "Blessed are they who suffer persecution for justice's sake," we know we are on the right path.

"If any of you have a son or an ox and he falls into a pit, will he not immediately rescue him on the sabbath day?" This they could not answer. And they never will.

# Humility

LUKE 14:1, 7-11

*Saturday of the Thirtieth Week of the Year*

Jesus is at it again practicing his special brand of table ministry. His lesson for the guests is humility as he chides them for seeking the places of honor at the table. Jesus tells us that those who exalt themselves will be humbled, while those who humble themselves will be exalted.

It will be also at a table where Jesus will teach the final lesson on humility when he washes the feet of the apostles. In this extraordinary gesture, Jesus set the tone and direction of what the church was supposed to be. Two thousand years later, we still look to that event as the standard of what a Christian's life should be like and what ministry in the church should reflect.

We have never, as a church, scored one hundred percent on the humility report card, and I don't think we ever will. Still, we struggle, and we try to be faithful to the example and call of Jesus to be his humble little rag-tag band of foot washers trying to transform the world, not by force or power or influence, but by love.

When we, the church, succeed, it is so beautiful. When we encounter individuals whose whole life is given to loving service to their families, the poor, children, etc., it is breathtaking. History has taught us that the only thing that works is being what Jesus calls us to be—poor, humble servants in love with the world and dedicated to serving God's people.

When a person tries to live this way, they are always in the place of honor, because the place of honor is one's heart. When one knows that they are doing God's work by serving God's people, they enjoy the most beautiful and most wonderful peace. They know that everything they have is a gift of a loving God. Their joy is to give that gift and share their life with others. They know their gifts and talents and never deny them. They also know who gave them their gifts.

This loving humility does not mean acting like a mole who feels inferior and unimportant. The humble person feels very important because there is no one else quite like them and there is no one else who can do the job that they are called to do. Humility has to do with knowing that the greater one's gifts are, the greater is the responsibility of using them in service for the entire body of Christ.

## Hospitality

### LUKE 14:12-14

*Monday of the Thirty-First Week of the Year*

The beggars, the crippled, the lame, and the blind are supposed to be the guests at our tables. How infrequently they are. Jesus is calling us to a whole new way of welcoming and sharing our life with the poor and the unwanted.

Jesus is calling us to have real compassion and to show kindness to those who are ordinarily excluded. In every parish, there are always people who are odd and trying. They always show up at all the special events. They can be loud and intrusive. They can try your patience.

It's always at the most inconvenient time that someone comes looking for a handout. It's not just the handout, but the need they have to tell some long tale that's usually a fabrication. It will always be a poor soul who tries to monopolize your time when you're greeting people after Mass or at a meeting. They will volunteer to do things they can't possibly accomplish. People like this can drive you crazy.

And yet, isn't the church supposed to be the place where they can go? Didn't they go to Jesus, and didn't he always find time and have patience? Sometimes I can get so taken up with the doing of church business, programs, and liturgy that I forget the most important thing I can ever do is to take the time to really look at the person, really listen to them and truly be present.

The little act of kindness and patience done to one of the little ones means more than all the liturgies and programs we could ever have. What a wonderful credit it is to the church that the "little ones" do find a place and a home. When we open our hearts and arms to them, all kind of blessings come to us.

We know we are on the right track when we treat the poorest of the poor with the same respect that we extend to the biggest contributor to the parish. The teaching of Jesus about the "widow's mite" is valid on many different levels.

## The Parable of the Great Banquet

LUKE 14:15-24

*Tuesday of the Thirty-First Week of the Year*

This beautiful gospel of the Messianic banquet tells us that the poor and humble will have the first places with Jesus. The image of the dinner party or the banquet describes the Kingdom of God, the church, and the eucharist.

What is so appealing about this story is the universality of God's love and the welcome given to all who are invited to the banquet. The servants of the master are sent out to invite and welcome all to the table. The master is not satisfied until there is a house full of guests. The master represents our loving Father, who wills the salvation and life of all people. He sets up no barrier, but his arms are open to all.

You and I are the beneficiaries of the loving mercy and kindness of our Father. We know so well our unworthiness, and yet the Father overlooks it all and welcomes us as his precious and beloved children. As we reflect on this beautiful passage, it is so obvious that God's plan is for those who have accepted the invitation to then become in turn the extenders of the invitation to others. We who are so hungry have found the Living Bread, the very life of Jesus Christ, in the eucharist. The joy of our life becomes the sharing of this bread with others who are also hungry again. We do not hoard the bread. Rather we break it and share it with our sisters and brothers.

The meaning of our lives will be expressed in how generously and lovingly we share the bread of life and love. When we are generous in sharing who and what we are, we are never hungry. We are always satisfied and filled. The more we give away, the more baskets of bread are left over to feed ourselves and the whole world.

The sad part of this gospel is the story of those who were, and are today, invited to the banquet but who turn down the invitation. Someone or something seems to be more wonderful than Jesus. But that could never be. Unfortunately so many who were invited but declined, go through life never knowing or appreciating what God has in store for them. Instead of being fulfilled and joyful guests at the table, they become the poor and dejected hungry paupers who could have had everything if only they had said "yes" to the invitation.

# The Cost of Discipleship

LUKE 14:25-33

*Wednesday of the Thirty-First Week of the Year*

It costs a lot to follow Jesus. Placing Jesus before our family, flesh and blood, friends, career, dreams, and plans is demanded and expected of the disciple. Jesus tells us we must take up our cross and follow after him.

The image of building the tower is a good example of what discipleship involves. We don't just say we'd like to build a tower or simply begin to build; we have to plan, get materials, devote hours and hours of work, and of course, we have to have the money to pay for the project. We have to be willing to pay the price of what the building will demand of our time, talents, and treasure.

To be the Lord's disciple also demands knowing what it will cost to be one and being willing to pay the price. The price is the dying to what is not of the Lord's Kingdom in our hearts and being willing to follow in the Master's footsteps each day. To follow Jesus demands a daily walk with him. It means being willing to allow the Lord to enter into all the areas of our life, especially the most personal. Our vocation, family, career, pursuits, hobbies, talents—everything is a part of the gift we must make to the Lord. There are no areas in which we prevent him from entering.

Christian discipleship is so much more than the saying of prayers or following of religious practices. It demands that our hearts, our lives, our very souls are open to the Lord. It means that there is nothing that is "mine." Everything is God's.

Words are easy and cheap. Being his disciple demands so much more. It demands action. It demands a whole life lived for him, holding nothing back. It's fine to say that we want to be his; it's quite another thing to live and act that way in all the areas of our lives.

We need to invite the Lord's spirit into our hearts so that we can follow through and make a reality of that which we say we are—a disciple of Jesus Christ. As we rely more and more on the Spirit, it becomes easier to "walk the walk" and not just "talk the talk."

## The Parables of the Lost Sheep and the Lost Coin

LUKE 15:1-10

*Thursday of the Thirty-First Week of the Year*

How much Jesus loves the sinner, the outcast, and the poor! He welcomes them and even eats with them. This is Jesus' great crime and unforgivable sin. He eats with sinners. In Jesus' culture, he says by this eucharistic activity that he wants to be in loving communication with them. What Jesus does is an act of intimacy. How can one be intimate with the scum of the earth? How can the Son of God seem to enjoy breaking bread with those who are sinners and those who have been thrown out of the synagogue and society? Jesus is there for those who really need him—the sinners.

Wouldn't you love to be a fly on the wall during one of those meals? Imagine the salty language! Imagine the tall tales of the prostitute and the tax collectors! They have seen it all, and then some!

I think Jesus was there at table because he really wanted to be and because he genuinely enjoyed himself. I don't think he talked much about the Temple gossip or about religious topics or even about his Father. I think what Jesus did at a dinner party was eat and enjoy the meal and some local wine. I think he was totally present to the people at table. He listened and he responded. He joked and he laughed. He also cried when that was appropriate.

The guests at table with Jesus were struck and touched by his genuine humanity and the real love that flowed from him to them. They felt, they knew, that he really loved them and that he was so happy to be with them. He wasn't there to convince, convert, or judge. He was there to have a good time with people he respected and liked.

The magnetism and power of Jesus is his pure and sincere love for everyone. He excludes no one. He looks down on no one. He disrespects no one. He condemns no one.

Isn't this someone that that you would like to have a meal with? Wouldn't you like to sit next to him at table and listen and speak with him? He invites us to join him at the table of eucharist. We are his special guests. He wants us by his side. He delights when we will accept the bread of life from him. Even though we are not worthy, we know we are always welcome.

## The Parable of the Dishonest Manager

LUKE 16:1-8

*Friday of the Thirty-First Week of the Year*

Jesus referred to the rich man's manager as being enterprising. We would probably call him a crook. In reality, that's what he was. First of all, he dissipated his master's property. That means theft, mismanagement, waste, and fraud. When the boss gives him the "pink slip," he then ponders his future. He's not interested in normal ways of supporting himself, like work, so he devises a grand scheme which will guarantee that he will always have entrée to the rich and famous peoples' homes. He cheats in their favor by reducing their indebtedness to the boss. Quite a guy, this manager!

What does Jesus praise about this fellow? His initiative, creativity, and brains, not his dishonesty. What

Jesus is commenting on is that when it comes to worldly or dishonest pursuits, people like the manager run rings about the church.

Isn't it strange that we who have the greatest thing the world has ever known, Jesus Christ, present him in such a way that we put people to sleep with our half-hearted, unenthusiastic, and boring presentations? Advertisers will spend any amount, go to any length, and make any necessary sacrifice to sell a tube of toothpaste, and we present the Lord in ways that can often insult intelligent people. We don't seem to look for exciting and creative ways to sell him. We often follow a "take it" or "leave it" attitude to the way we communicate the best news the world has to offer.

If we are not excited about our Jesus, if we are not enthusiastic about our marriage, priesthood, or conse-crated life, how do we ever expect to excite other people? Isn't it time that we learn to share our treasure—Jesus—with other people? Isn't it time the church began to use the most brilliant and creative people around to create new ways of introducing Jesus to a world that's hunger-ing for him?

If you come upon that manager, grab him and give him a job with the church in evangelization, but just keep your eye on him!

## The World's Goods

LUKE 16:9-15

*Saturday of the Thirty-First Week of the Year*

This passage from Luke continues Jesus' teaching on money and material things, a subject often spoken about by Jesus. Jesus advises the disciples to make friends for themselves through their use of this world's goods so that when they fail, the disciples will find a wel-come reception in people's homes.

Jesus is teaching the value of honesty, stewardship, and charity. The honest person is always respected and honored. That person who is always just and fair with all creates a relationship of deep respect and honor with other people. That kind of living is marked by a proper use of things. Things never become an end in themselves, but only a means of caring for one's family and achieving modest and proper dignity and security. For such a person, profit is not the highest priority, people are. The honest person is the person of charity who realizes that everything they possess is a gift of God and that there is a solemn duty and responsibility to share that gift with those who have little or nothing of the world's wealth.

It is always so touching to receive checks in the mail from people who have been blessed that are "for a poor family," "for a kid in jail," "for someone in trouble," "for a kid's tuition," etc. What a blessing it is when people know that they have been blessed and act accordingly.

What about you and me and our honesty, integrity, and charity? How much of our blessing do we share? Are we habitually caring for someone who has little? Are we at the bedside of our sick friend? Do we coach a basketball game or teach a CCD class? What are we doing to share the treasure the Lord has given to us?

Are we serving two masters? We can't. It will destroy us. We find our peace when we give ourselves completely to the One Master, the Lord Jesus. When we do that, then there are no other masters. Everything in our life is in order. Remember Jesus' words—"You justify yourselves in the eyes of people, but God reads your hearts."

# Sin and Faith

*Monday of the Thirty-Second Week of the Year*

Today's gospel speaks to us about scandals and faith—strange bedfellows. In particular, Jesus speaks of giving scandal to the little ones. He tells us it would be better that a millstone be tied around our necks and we be thrown into the sea than we hurt his little ones in any way.

What a privilege and responsibility it is to be a parent or to be in any way responsible for children. Today's world demands that parents be such special people completely dedicated to their children. But we need a more developed spirituality of parenthood. It is such a special calling.

To be a parent is like being God. To cooperate in bringing life into this world and to nurture that life and care for it is so sacred, so holy, and so God-like. When parents deny themselves and do anything for their children's well-being, they are doing the holiest of all the works of the church. They are literally writing the next chapter of the story of the human family as they form their children to know and love God. As the children experience the love of their parents, they learn that they are God's precious children.

These are not good days for the little ones. In the society of today, there are so many people after them. Children are the victims of poverty, hunger, abuse, abortion, and war. They work in factories at early ages to produce designer products for the western world. They are sexual commodities in many cultures, suffering from everything from victimization in media and the modeling profession to pornography and prostitution.

It is the sacred duty of the church and the world to protect these precious ones and not allow anyone to hurt them.

When the family, the church, and society can create a world with the faith that Jesus speaks of, we have an environment in which they will be cherished and respected. What a heartbreak it is to find so many parents who *never* bring their children to church, *never* teach them about God, *never* teach them to pray. To fail to give the gift of faith is the very real scandal that Jesus condemns.

## The Attitude of a Servant

LUKE 17:7-10

*Tuesday of the Thirty-Second Week of the Year*

"We are useless servants. We have done no more than our duty." It takes a holy person to say such a thing. It takes great humility and a great sense of mission to mean those words. Every so often we come upon someone who is totally and completely filled with a sense of God's presence and love. When we meet someone like that, we know that we are in another realm. We stand on holy ground in their presence.

People like this are so filled with a sense of wonder and joy that God loves them so much he called them by name and allows them to care for part of his little flock. People like this—mothers and fathers, priests, young adults, senior citizens—possess a sense of joy and happiness that is contagious. They simply can't believe that God has so honored them to be servants of the flock.

Somewhere along the line, they understood the meaning of the Washing of the Feet. They live it day in and day out. They look for no praise or recognition in what they do. They are so happy and honored to be God's "useless servants."

I remember meeting some of these "useless servants" in the sisters I met who staff orphanages in El Salvador. I saw in them a poverty and openness to God's love that caused one to weep in their presence because God was so powerfully present. Their beloved children were always around them. The children obviously loved their sisters, and the sisters returned the compliment. The places were poor, yet they were on holy ground because God was there.

I think of another special "useless servant," a young mother of a three-year-old boy. She has nothing and no one except her beloved son, and her church that she loves so much and which loves her back. Her whole life is totally given to try to survive and to give her son what he needs. She gives him the most important thing—pure, selfless love. She is God's love to her son. She is a saint.

The sisters and this single mother would say the same thing: "We have done no more than our duty."

## The Cleansing of Ten Lepers

LUKE 17:11-19

*Wednesday of the Thirty-Second Week of the Year*

"One leper, realizing that he had been cured, came back praising God in a loud voice." I wonder if the reasons that the other nine did not return to thank Jesus for their cure was that they didn't realize they had been cured.

Sometimes we become so used to our infirmity and our personal leprosy that even when the Lord touches us and heals us, we don't know it, or worse, we don't want it. We get used to the old ways, and it's easy to stay with them. When we remain in the old, we will never be challenged or bothered. After all, saying, "I can't" do this or that absolves us from being part of many things, and it frees us from having to go out of ourselves to help others.

Very often when we say, "I can't," what we really mean is, "I don't want to." When we have that attitude, it is impossible for the healing grace of Jesus to really have an effect on our lives and on our emotions. When we choose sickness of body, mind, or spirit, we are choosing to limit the power of Christ in our lives, and we are deciding how much of the Christ life we will live.

We are actually able to limit the life and depth of the Lord in our life. We can set limits as to how much and how effectively he can help us or be part of us. We determine by our attitude the extent that Jesus will be allowed to be part of our real life.

The healing touch of Jesus is the beginning of transformation and change. We have to determine whether we really want to be touched and changed. We have to determine how much we wish to allow the Lord into our life.

Like the leper in the gospel, we have to mean it when we cry out to Jesus to have mercy on us and make us clean. We also have to be ready to return to him in joy to give him thanks and to change our life.

## The Kingdom of God

LUKE 17:20-25

*Thursday of the Thirty-Second Week of the Year*

"The reign of God is already in your midst!" This news astounds the scribes and Pharisees, but they obviously don't believe it. It's too easy. It's available for everybody. Everyone is included. No one is excluded. This can't be the Kingdom!

The same feelings are echoed today in the church when it comes to salvation and God's love. The Kingdom dwells within us. It is not something to be obtained, but rather something to be accepted. The scriptures and teachings of the church are clear and to the point. The

Holy Spirit dwells within us through baptism. The life of God is given to us.

Our life's challenge and pursuit is to accept and live what has already been given to us. We already possess God. God is not "out there" somewhere to be tracked down, located, and conquered. God is the willing victim who is there for us for the taking. God is not far away. God is within.

Today so many good people go to the four corners of the earth to find God. They believe that God is *really* present at some shrine where an apparition of Mary has taken place. They believe that some holy place will provide them with the gift of God and God's peace.

But the Lord is always with them, waiting for them to accept and love the God who dwells in their hearts in faith. The Lord is constantly available and present in the community, the body of Christ, in the word of God, the sacraments, and above all, in the eucharist. What more can the Lord give us? He has already given us himself. There is nothing more to give. He died on the cross for us and rose from the dead.

When we go to church or when we take a trip to a shrine or holy place, it renews our faith, but there is nothing more there that God can give us. The value of church and these places is that they remind us of what we already possess, which is God—in other words, everything.

The reign of God *is* already in our midst.

# The Day of the Son of Man

LUKE 17:26-37

*Friday of the Thirty-Second Week of the Year*

The Son of Man is going to come, and when he returns he will establish his justice. You'd better be ready. You don't know when or where or how. But you can be sure of it. He is coming.

Is there anyone who doesn't think about his or her death? Is there anyone who isn't a little afraid of the prospect of judgment when every part of our hearts and all of our actions will be revealed? Of course we are a bit apprehensive if we're normal.

The Lord does tell us to be prepared. How does one get ready for the Lord's return, the end of the world, and their own personal death? We get ready for all of that by living today with all the love and faith we can muster up.

All we have is today. Yesterday is beyond our control and tomorrow doesn't exist yet. But today is right here before me. I have the ability of this day. I can choose to love or hate. I can help or hurt. I can believe or doubt. I can hope or despair. I can live for others or I can live just for myself. The whole day is filled with so many opportunities to love and choose God.

The only way that I can be ready for the Lord's return is to make myself so busy doing the right thing that I don't have time to think of anything except doing what he wants of me. Salvation and life is not a question of being afraid and dreading his coming; it's a process of being so consumed in his love that when he does come we won't even know it because we'll be so busy helping a sister or brother.

Salvation is work. It's living for other people. It's being always busy building a little bit of the Kingdom. When we live like that, we have no interest or time to be afraid of his return because he is already here. We have met him, loved him, and cared for him in all the little sisters and brothers that we love and serve. When he calls, we may have to say to him: "Wait a minute, Lord, I am taking care of your little brother!"

## The Parable of the Persistent Widow

LUKE 18:1-8

*Saturday of the Thirty-Second Week of the Year*

How blessed we are if we have people in our lives like the widow in today's gospel praying for us! There are pray-ers, and there are pray-ers. When we can latch on to some of the special pray-ers, we know that everything will work out and be okay.

I have people in my life that I know love to drive God crazy. They are unrelenting in prayer. They never give up. They are like the drop of water that wears the rock and stone away until the Grand Canyon appears. Even if it takes millions of years, they don't care. They will stick to their prayer and wear God down just the way the widow did to the unjust judge.

When I'm in a lot of trouble, I make a phone call to one of my special pray-ers. When I do, I know I'm in good hands.

Praying for another is such a special privilege. When someone asks you to pray for them, take it very seriously because it is a very serious matter. Another person is placing their soul in your hands for safe keeping. When we promise to pray, it is a very special trust. I know people who have hundreds of names on their prayer list, and they look at them and touch them during their prayer time.

What a grace it is when we are all connected and united to the great Pray-er—the Priest, Jesus. All our hearts and all our prayers become one as we pray in and through him to the Father in the unity of the Holy Spirit.

When we enter the beautiful realm of intercessory prayer we have extended the Kingdom in a very special way because we are doing the priestly work of Jesus by being lovingly united with all his sisters and brothers. Take very seriously the promise: "I'll pray for you." Ask with deep faith and gratitude: "Please pray for me."

## A Blind Man Receives His Sight

LUKE 18:35-43

*Monday of the Thirty-Third Week of the Year*

"Jesus, Son of David, have pity on me!" The blind man in today's gospel prays for the first time the great and powerful Jesus prayer—a prayer which has echoed down the centuries countless times. It is in many ways the perfect prayer, the prayer of total abandonment to the mercy of God.

What makes this prayer so powerful is its complete sincerity. The blind man has sat on that same road for years. He has lived a dark and isolated life. His only hope is to receive a coin that will buy him some food for the day.

Many people pass by each day. One thing that he gets is plenty of gossip. Strangers are always talking about what's happening in Jericho and Jerusalem. He's heard a lot about this wonderful rabbi named Jesus. They say that he even heals people. Each day Jesus is always in the conversations the blind beggar overhears.

Then finally one day, Jesus, surrounded by a crowd, passes the beggar on the road. The blind beggar realizes this is his chance, that Jesus may never pass by him again. He musters up all his courage and strength and shouts at the top of his voice: "Jesus, Son of David, have pity on me!" And Jesus stops and asks to see him.

That poor man shouted out to Jesus because he was desperate. He knew he had no other chance at life. He had to shout right then or for sure he would spend the rest of his life in darkness begging by the side of the road. "I want to see, Lord." "Receive your sight. Your faith has healed you." And the man began a new life.

Have you ever prayed with the passion and sincerity of this poor man? Have you ever poured your whole heart and soul into your prayer so that Jesus knew you really wanted it? Don't we usually pray in a very laid-back and reserved way so that if we don't get what we asked for we won't be too disappointed or upset because we really didn't expect it in the first place?

Maybe someday our prayer will have the abandonment of the blind beggar and we will shout out: "Jesus, Son of David, have pity on me."

## Jesus and Zacchaeus

LUKE 19:1-10

*Tuesday of the Thirty-Third Week of the Year*

Hello, Zacchaeus! What a treat it is to read this gospel. Zacchaeus is such a likeable man. He knows what he wants, and he goes after it even if it means climbing a tree. While the gospel tells us that he was "small of stature," I imagine him as being large of girth. So the scene of him climbing a tree and seating himself on a branch has to be a sight to see.

But Zacchaeus does something that we all have to do. He was unable to see Jesus because of the crowd towering around him and blocking his view. Most of us also have difficulty seeing Jesus because many things block out our vision of him. Jobs, responsibilities, families, concerns, problems, and projects—there are any number of things, some of them good and even holy, that can block our view of Jesus. That's why we have to climb our sycamore tree so we get a fresh view and a little space to think and to see. That's what our daily reading of the gospel and prayer time is meant to do. We need to get a little perspective so that the responsibilities of our lives, as good as they are, don't overwhelm us to the point that we can't see Jesus any more.

A little bit of quiet time, even driving in the car or having a cup of coffee with the phone off the hook, is able to refresh us so that we can go back to our family and work with a clearer vision and the ability to love and give a little more.

There is no question about it, a daily routine of even just a few minutes of conversation with Jesus directs and influences our whole day. We will be more present to our loved ones the more we have given ourselves the opportunity to be present to Jesus. We will relate better to people and work harder and better the more Jesus has been allowed to enter our personal life through prayer.

Zacchaeus was a lucky man. Jesus wanted to come to his home to eat with him. That meant he wanted to be intimate with him. We are lucky, too, for Jesus wants to sit down at table and sup with us in the eucharist of his life and love. "Zacchaeus, come down!"

## The Parable of the Ten Gifts

LUKE 19:11-28

*Wednesday of the Thirty-Third Week of the Year*

We deal with a hard man as king in today's gospel. I can't picture him as the merciful Lord who is so forgiving, even when we sit down and do nothing with what the Lord has given to us. Nonetheless, we all have a great lesson to learn in this gospel: we will be judged by how we have used the gifts the Lord has given, not because the Lord needs the results, but the community does. We are given gifts of talent, personality, understanding, abilities, powers to heal and comfort, gifts of teaching, preaching, leadership, and counseling not for the Lord's benefit, but for the benefit of our sisters and brothers.

When we sit back and settle for less than we know we can be, we hurt not God, but ourselves and our dear sisters and brothers. How sad it is to see someone who has "just settled," when they could have become so much more for themselves and for the community.

We also know that as one really works at becoming what they are called to be, more gifts are given them. The more a person grows in mind, spirit, soul, and body, the more capable that person becomes of growing more and receiving more of God's graces and blessings.

Have you settled? Have you come to the point (even in success) when you say enough is enough? Have you reached the point where you think there's no more to learn—you've seen it all? Our God has created us a little less than himself. He has blessed us with so many gifts of mind and soul and spirit. They are always growing and always hungry for more because they are searching for God.

This gospel unsettles us because we love to create for ourselves safe havens where we are not challenged or upset. The God of surprises likes to upset the apple cart and call us out of our comfort zone. It would be so embarrassing to appear before the Lord at the end of the journey and hand him back only what he gave us at the beginning. If we run with him and trust him, the gifts and talents will multiply and our arms will be laden with gifts to give him. Don't be afraid to try!

# Jesus Weeps Over Jerusalem

LUKE 19:41-44

*Thursday of the Thirty-Third Week of the Year*

This gospel of the destruction of Jerusalem is very sad. Jesus is begging for his people to hear his voice and change while there is still time. We have to listen to that voice too. We have to be sure that we are not allowing destructive tendencies to cripple us permanently.

Jesus preached a beautiful gospel of forgiveness and reconciliation, and his church continues to preach this beautiful message of hope. But we must make a distinction between the forgiveness of sins and the effects of sin in our lives. That is why the church has to preach about the horror of sin along with the merciful forgiveness of God no matter what we do.

I think of people who have destroyed their marriages or their priesthood or religious profession because of illicit involvement. Homes and families have been ruined and tremendous sorrow and pain have been inflicted on innocent people because of the actions of otherwise very good people. No question that the Lord lovingly embraced and forgave these good people, but they had to live with the pain they caused to others for the rest of their lives.

No ministry of the church is more Christ-like than that of reaching out in love and merciful forgiveness to those who have had an abortion. So many of these poor souls are more victims themselves than doers of evil. Yet they often live with the burden to what they have done to their little baby. As often as the church tells them they are forgiven, they are unable to forgive themselves because the guilt is so terrible and the yearning for their baby so great.

Those who have destroyed their lives and others' because of drug or alcohol abuse receive God's loving forgiveness, but often live with the ghosts of people or relationships they have destroyed. Indeed, one of the steps of AA is to repair the hurts and pain the person has caused because of drinking or drug abuse.

It is a hard concept, isn't it—the total and complete forgiveness of our sins by a merciful and loving God, along with the life-long effects of some actions in our lives and the lives of others?

Let's pray that we, along with the people of Jerusalem, can hear the warning of Jesus to leave the ways of evil and return to him so that we will not be harmed in any way and will always be safe.

Let's also pray for those sisters and brothers who continue to pay for sins long ago forgiven. They are usually such good and holy people. Isn't it a bit unfair that some of us can luxuriate in God's forgiveness while others never stop praying over their sin?

## The Cleansing of the Temple

LUKE 19:45-48

*Friday of the Thirty-Third Week of the Year*

"B-14! Please take your chance on the Super Bonanza! There's still time to take a brick in the Millennium Fund! Please take a pledge in the Bishop's Appeal! The Rosary-Altar Society is selling cakes after all the masses! The K of C is selling chances on a new car after the Masses. Please don't forget to buy your SCRIP for the benefit of the school."

I'm sure that these announcements from St. Brigid's Church are just like the ones from your church. I'm also sure that your pastor winces the way I do on the Sunday this gospel is read, followed by one of the above announcements!

Is the church a den of thieves as Jesus said the temple was? Is the church the place of prayer that Jesus said the temple was meant to be? Is money a part of God's house and worship for the church? Tough questions aren't they? But here's a tougher one still: Are you and I thieves by the way we keep back from God what is rightfully God's?

There are certainly parishes that are run in the "den of thieves" spirit. They are constantly asking for money. They do so because they never truly talk about the responsibility each of us has in supporting the church in true sacrificial giving. In place of educating, challenging, and inspiring their people to give, they constantly nickel and dime them with many tasteless ways to squeeze another dollar rather than to call them to real generosity.

Contributions will greatly reflect the scriptural and prayer life of the community. In a spirit-based parish, God's people are being called to be what they truly are—church.

Pastors must honestly ask themselves if they are prostitutes themselves by not accepting the call to educate and call their people to sacrificial giving in the spirit of tithing. But while we're on the subject, our people have to get over this stingy-mindedness in which the average Catholic gives less than 1.1% of their earnings to the church, making it almost the lowest priority in the family budget.

## Marriage and the Resurrection

LUKE 20:27-40

*Saturday of the Thirty-Third Week of the Year*

In today's gospel we hear the puzzling and somewhat amazing story of the lady who married the seven brothers after each of the predecessors' demise. The question was: "At the resurrection, whose wife will she be?" I think the question really should have been: "Why hasn't this lady been canonized after having been wife to seven brothers?" She's incredible, and she deserves the Academy Award for patience and perseverance!

Kidding aside, this story is really the dispute between the Sadduccees and the scribes about the resurrection and life after death. Jesus beautifully reminds his hearers that his Father is the Father of the living, not the dead. The question does touch a very deep place in people's hearts when they ask if they will be with and know their loved ones who have died when they themselves get to heaven. The answer, of course, is the loudest and most joyful "Yes!"

While we will relate in a very different way in the presence of God, we will certainly know and love one another in a more perfect and complete way than we have ever known on earth. Heaven is really God. God is the fullness of perfect love.

God has created us for himself. God has destined us to be forever part of the mystery of love of the Holy Trinity. The closest we ever come to that perfect love of God on earth is when we love one another. Human love, however, is only a hint of the love that we will know when we are totally possessed by God.

The good lady of today's gospel will not love seven husbands or be wife to them as she was on earth. She will know them and love them in a more perfect way than she ever dreamt of on earth. All the imperfection of human loving and all the weaknesses of our personality will be made perfect when we are one in the passionate and perfect love of God.

What equips us here on earth, as the popular line from the musical Les Misérables tells us is, "to love another person is to see the face of God"—here on earth and when we get home to God.

# The Widow's Mite

### LUKE 21:1-4

*Monday of the Last Week of the Year*

The story of the Widow's Mite is more than a lesson in generosity; it is really a challenge to give Jesus everything, not just what we own but who we are.

As the widow holds back nothing, she challenges us to look into our own hearts and see what we are holding on to and not willing to part with. One day Mother Teresa was speaking to a group of high-powered and wealthy business people. They were very moved by her talk and asked with great sincerity what they could do to help her work. They of course meant: "How much?" She responded by telling them to go home and really love their spouses and children. She was calling on them to give their hearts to their family. That means presence, tenderness, time, listening, speaking, praying, and building the family of God. It's much easier to write a check.

Another time a group was so moved by her words that they pledged to give her anything to run her soup kitchen. She responded by asking them to volunteer to serve the hungry at the kitchen first. Mother Teresa, who had given the Lord and the poorest of the poor her widow's mite, was challenging these people and us to give to the Lord what he really seeks—our hearts and our love.

The Lord looks for this gift to be given to our own dear families and friends and to all people, especially the poor, the unloved, the sick, and the lonely. There are so many people who are doing this each and every day of their lives. There are saints in our parishes who care for the sick and physically and emotionally challenged. Their love is such a blessing to the whole body of Christ.

The gospel of the Widow's Mite is a very strong challenge to what we do with our time, money, possessions, gifts, and talents. Are we generous in sharing them with the Lord and his people, or are we cheap, keeping things for ourselves and never giving away anything that we will ever feel? Have we given our hearts completely to the Lord or to anyone else? May the poor widow, along with Mother Teresa, pray for us today for generosity of spirit.

## The Destruction of the Temple Foretold

LUKE 21:5-11

*Tuesday of the Last Week of the Year*

The gospels for the remainder of this last week in ordinary time will be speaking of the end of the world, the end times and the rapture. In today's gospel we see Jesus responding to the comments of the people about the beauty and the glory of the Temple in Jerusalem. The Temple meant so much to the national and religious identity and pride of the people. It was so large and so magnificent, a truly worthy place to house the Ark of the Covenant. Much of the activity and economic health of Jerusalem revolved around the daily schedule of worship and sacrifice of the Temple. The Temple was also a statement of pride to the Romans and to all others that we are an important people. But it all came down, and all that's left is the Wailing Wall.

The message of Jesus is very clear: "God is a God of the Spirit. He *may* raise buildings, but he doesn't *need* them." Unfortunately, we need them, and we sometimes try to use them as a way of controlling God or keeping God in his place.

Just look at all the buildings the church built in the fifties—seminaries, convents, novitiates, schools, rectories, and churches. Many of them are closed now. Parishes are being combined. A church that was once so powerful has been humbled. Perhaps as we pray over this gospel we can find consolation and meaning.

Whenever we make God subservient to structures, buildings, finances, pastoral structures, and planning, we run into trouble. The church *needs* money and resources. It needs buildings and staff persons. It cannot do the Lord's work without these things. But what is most important? Is everything we have used to serve the Lord and minister to his people, especially the poor? Is the first priority *always* the building up of the Kingdom?

When our hearts are with the Lord, it doesn't matter if St. Peter's and all the other buildings come tumbling down. Nothing has happened to the church. We, the little flock huddled together in Jesus' love, are the true church. Nothing will ever happen to us, for Jesus is with us, and he will never abandon us.

## The Coming Persecution

LUKE 21:12-19

*Wednesday of the Last Week of the Year*

Today, Jesus warns us about persecutions, violence, trials, and even death. It is a very sobering picture to consider as we come to the end of the year and reflect upon the "last things."

But, Jesus assures us that he will give us the words and wisdom, which our adversaries can take exception to or contradict.

These words were very real to me in the summer of 1998 when I visited the holy land of El Salvador. This tortured and holy land has been the scene of many martyrdoms—the Jesuits at the University of Central America, the American sisters, Archbishop Romero, and thousands of others whose names we do not even know. They all knew that their lives were in danger, yet they never stopped doing their jobs and helping their people.

They preached the gospel by the way they lived their lives. They saw Jesus in the poor and they were faithful to Him to the end.

I wonder what they thought about when they read this Gospel. I wonder if they told Jesus that they couldn't do it, that they were afraid, and that this was too much for them. I wonder if they thought about being quiet, or even getting another assignment and getting out of the country? I wonder if they complained to the Lord that this was all so unfair? Here they were risking their lives, and so many other priests and religious were living in the lap of luxury in North America, far removed from their daily fears and struggles.

So how did they do it? They got the grace they needed to hold on and not abandon their people. They believed that the Lord would see them through it. And he did.

When you visit the holy places when they worked and died, you know you are on holy earth. The people regard them as their saints. They were the ones who loved them even to the point of laying down their lives.

I had the incredible honor of celebrating mass for my young people at the altar where Archbishop Romero was martyred. "The good shepherd lays down his life for the flock" (John 10). Few times has the Mass meant so much for me than that holy moment when I stood in the footsteps of Oscar Romero. May his spirit guide us.

## The End Times

LUKE 21:20-28

*Thursday of the Last Week of the Year*

In today's gospel we read of the destination of Jerusalem and the end of the world. It is frightening stuff. The only consoling note is the coming of the Son of Man to bring salvation and life to all people.

As I read this gospel, I can't help but think that as terrible as these scenes of the end of the world are, compared to what millions of people have already gone through, they seem like small potatoes.

Let us just remember the hell that we have brought to one another. Think of the atomic bombs that were dropped on Japan, the Holocaust, the Second World War, Vietnam, ethnic cleansing, etc. Humans themselves have produced scenes of hell, destruction, torture, and death far worse than even the most apocalyptic scenes from the scriptures. We have outdone even the Lord in terms of human punishment and suffering. We have done it to ourselves, and we show every promise of not stopping.

Perhaps this gospel could serve as a warning to all of us that we must wage peace and justice. It is never God's plan or will that the human family should suffer through wars and persecution.

Advent will soon be with us and with it the promise of new beginnings and new life. We are not condemned by our past. There is still time to hammer our swords into pruning hooks. There is still the possibility of the lamb and the lion lying down in peace and friendship.

We pray so fervently for peace. Imagine the new Garden of Eden that could grow as we use our resources, not for armaments but for schools, decent housing, and drug rehabilitation programs. Imagine that Garden of Eden as we remove all the land mines and close the School of the Americas.

This gospel tells us that the world should end only once, and until that day comes, this beautiful earth is meant to be the new Garden of Eden where all people, regardless of race, religion, nationality, and language will be one family sharing all the gifts of the loving God.

# The Lesson of the Fig Tree

### LUKE 21:29-33

*Friday of the Last Week of the Year*

Today, Jesus invites us to look at the fig tree. When it begins to bud, we know that summer is near. Jesus is speaking of signs to indicate that the reign of God is near.

Perhaps we can also use this scripture to remind ourselves that we read the signs of the times in our own lives.

Our God is constantly making himself known to us in the events and the days and the stages of our lives. The Lord speaks to us in very different ways when we are young compared to when we are old. In all the stages of our lives, the Lord is speaking to us in a new, different, exciting, and challenging way.

Let's begin with the young person. College and early career days are days focused on ourselves, learning who we are and what we seek from life. All of that changes when the youth falls in love and marries. Parenthood brings demands, challenges, and joys that were never dreamt or anticipated. As parents watch their children grow, they are also given the opportunity to grow and become more of who they were meant to be. Middle age and becoming grandparents leads to retirement and old age, along with sickness, declining health, and the death of a spouse.

For others, a single life will be that path of one's life, and that will be filled with many different moments of growth and grace. Others will taste divorce, early widowhood, and single parenting. Each person's life will have so many turns and so many possibilities.

For the person of faith, each age and experience will be the opportunity for finding God. God's grace is with us in abundance no matter where we are in the journey. Let us not waste our lives wishing that the moment were other or different, but let us live it now, fully as it is and with all we are.

Indeed, *this* moment is our experience of the incarnation. All we have is this moment of grace in which Christ is totally present to us and for us. We cannot yearn for the past or hope for the future. We must live today experiencing every joy and pain, knowing that all we have is this moment to love and to be loved. For the believer, that is enough, for that is where God is.

## Be Vigilant

### LUKE 21:34-36

*Saturday of the Last Week of the Year*

This is the last day of the church's year of grace. Thank you so much for journeying with me these many weeks. These days are anything but "ordinary." Each day is like none other, filled with the opportunity to find God's love and presence. The daily opening of the word and the practice of *lectio divina* makes it much more likely that when God is present we will know it and act accordingly.

The final gospel of the year speaks about the final day and being ready for it. How will we be prepared to meet the Lord? How will we be prepared to die? The only way that makes sense to me is this: we must live every day as if it is our last. We can have no unfinished business. The house of our heart must be in order. We must forgive and accept forgiveness today. We will not wait until "whenever" to tell someone that we love him or her. We will share our love and friendship today. We will live passionately today. We will sing and dance and party when it is time. We will also mourn and weep when that is appropriate.

Being ready for the "end" means living this day in integrity, justice, truthfulness, mercy, and love. Our lives must be transparent. We can have no secret or hidden life. We have to live in complete scrutiny of the eye of the Lord and our community. We have to be people of the light, never fearing the darkness because we walk with the Lord.

It is my prayer that this book has helped you, and me, to get ready for death by encouraging us to live our lives fully and joyously in the presence of Jesus and the community. I also pray that you and I will turn to the gospel each day to discover anew the wonder of Jesus and to celebrate the love he has for us. As we live out our lives and our ministries, the word of God will direct, strengthen, affirm, and challenge us on the journey. The word will point us to Jesus like a sure compass.

"Jesus Christ, yesterday and today, the beginning and the end, the Alpha and the Omega! To him belong the days and the seasons. To him belongs all glory! Amen!" (Easter Vigil).

**Francis X. Gaeta** is pastor at St. Brigid's Church in Westbury, New York. Recently, Fr. Gaeta and the St. Brigid's community were the subject of a series of Pulitzer Prize winning articles by Bob Keeler published in *Newsday*, and later published in a book titled *Parish!* Fr. Gaeta is the author of four previous books including *From Holy Hour to Happy Hour*, *Come Celebrate Jesus*, *What He Did for Love*, and *The Great Fifty Days* (Resurrection Press).